PRAGUE BAROQUE ARCHITECTURE

Milan Pavlík and Vladimír Uher

THE PEPIN PRESS

ISBN 90 5496 013 2

A catalogue record for this book is available from the publishers
and from the Royal Dutch Library, The Hague

This book is edited, designed and produced by
The Pepin Press in Amsterdam and Kuala Lumpur.
Design: Pepin van Roojen and dorine van den Beukel
Editor: Dr Paul Wijdeveld
English copy editor: Rodney Bolt

The Pepin Press
P.O. Box 10349
1001 EH Amsterdam
The Netherlands
Fax (+) 31 20 4201152
Email: pepin@euronet.nl

Printed and bound in Singapore

On the front jacket: View into vault of vestibule and interior of Church of St Nicholas
On the back jacket: The Church of St Nicholas, stairs
Page 1: Černín Palace, design of the main hall decoration, Domenico Egidio Rossi, 1696
page 2: The Church of St Nicholas
Page 5: Lobkovic Palace, garden façade
Page 6: Archbishop's Palace

Contents

Preface

Over the past decade Czech Baroque, and Prague Baroque in particular, has been attracting increasing attention of art lovers and art historians. Part of the reason is that art history research has progressed substantially by the publication of works offering a comprehensive view (i.e. Franz, Bachmann, Blažíček, Neumann, Norberg-Schulz, *History of Czech Visual Arts*). The impressive outcome of these works, many of which might be called monumental, has advanced our knowledge to a point where a segment can be studied through detailed analysis without changing the contour. Thus the way for further research is opened up, raising challenging questions, and defining areas which have so far been vague. A team of researchers active at the State Institute for the Restoration of Historical Towns and Monuments (SURPMO), conducting a systematic architectural and historical survey of Prague, not only presented individual issues until now regarded as problematic, but also placed their results within a broader context. Nonetheless, many questions still remain open.

While art historians are fully justified in putting the main stress of their writings on defining the styles of art works, cataloguing the production of their makers, and determining their provenance, it has to be said that our knowledge still displays considerable gaps. Among many such examples is the ambiguity relating to the period of the Thirty Years War (1618-48), the cardinal problem of Czech art history. For a long time it has invited conflicting interpretations – the authorship of the dynamic group of structures dominated by the Břevnov Church, and the Church of St Nicholas in Malá Strana (The Lesser Quarter of Prague), the inability to document accurately some works of essential significance from the 17th and 18th centuries, or the dispute around the central issue of whether the concept of Baroque architecture is too broad to be applied to creations so full of contrasts as those of the 17th and 18th centuries (i.e. the relationship between Mannerism and Baroque in Prague).

In contrast to this historical approach, the general awareness is that historical architecture not only represents a source of knowledge about the past, but by its very existence consistently influences and shapes the spiritual aspect of the modern man, who enters into a dialogue both intentionally and spontaneously with the art of times long past. It seems that it is precisely modern architecture that has sharpened our senses and made them more perceptive of the qualities previously neglected; it provides new angles of vision for an evaluation of the historical development; the study of modern art and architecture helps us find analogies and parallels in the creation of the bygone ages and appreciate their remarkable achievements. However, we are so closely tied to our present-day lives that we manage to understand the artistic production of the past only in terms of its place in the present. The relativity of what can be called the present, and what is history, often makes things in the more distant past more comprehensible than those in a period just ended.

Understanding the values of historical architecture, therefore, is a constant regenerative process of art history work. It is an open system, which welcomes every new method of investigation, as long as it contributes in some way to grasping the content of a work of art. Therefore, perhaps, the interpretation of architectural compositions through artistic photography, also made possible by modern times, has its potential in revealing the rhythmic and optical values, the magic of structures and materials, and the beauty of shapes and their coalescence in works of architecture which form the daily scenery of our lives.

This book combines the experience of the present-day architect and photographer, who from their standpoint seek to explain the basic composition of Baroque architecture, i.e. the possibilities which always have been and will be available to the professional architect. For the architect will always deal with processing materials and structures, the shaping effects of light and shadow, rhythm and repetition, symmetry and asymmetry, and the tectonics and sculptural qualities of processed matter, as well as the use of scale, the choice of proportions and their combinations for achieving the desired effect. The wealth of Prague Baroque architecture compelled the authors to concentrate on only a limited selection of its aspects, namely the study of the composition of the matter, the surface area and the shape of the details.

The catalogue contains some new findings made through the authors' own research and drawn from the research work of the team of Dr. Dobroslav Líbal and the SURPMO.

It is him in particular that the authors wish to thank for his help and kind interest in this book. They value their cooperation of many years with Dr. Líbal on surveys and documentation of historical Prague in the SURPMO studio which he built up and led. Our thanks go also to our colleagues František Kašiška, Vladimír Pelzbauer and Josef Hyzler for providing us with background material for the pictorial part; and to the historian Luboš Lancinger, for long years of collaboration. The authors remember with esteem their late colleagues Jan Muk and Milada Vilímková, whose invaluable contribution to the knowledge of Prague's history has not yet been duly recognized as a number of the notes to the catalogue text will reveal.

Historical Background

At the end of the 16th century Prague had lost the splendour that it achieved when, during the Gothic age, it was the residence of Emperor Charles IV (1316-78), and became renowned throughout Europe. Having been built predominantly from brick and stone, the buildings of 14th century Prague could cope with the devastating effects of fires (such as the great fire of 1541), so that adaptations and changes did not affect the underlying structure. New buildings only supplemented the already generously conceived layout of the Gothic city and Renaissance styles from Italy, Germany and Holland that came up against local Gothic traditions succumbed. The perseverance of the Gothic age is perhaps most evident in the Church of St Roch in the Strahov Monastery, founded by Emperor Rudolf II and built in a Gothic style during the first decade of the 17th century (1603-12).

However, at the turn of the 16th into the 17th century, three buildings were erected which are interesting precisely for the implementation of new motifs. The oval ground-plans of the Vlašská (Italian) Chapel in the Jesuit Clementinum (1590-97), and the Matthias Portal of the Castle are perhaps not precursors of future Baroque formulae, but are already variations of early Baroque theoretical models (such as those by Serlio and Scamozzi). The third building – the rather small Church of the Holy Trinity (1611-14) – is marked by the wonderful compactness of the interior space, which results not so much from the ground-plan (nave with side niches), as from the proportions and the well-balanced architectural order.

The Battle of the White Mountain in 1620, the regrouping of internal and external political forces, and the general economic disruption during the Thirty Years War caused enduring changes in economic and political power. The imposing piles built for the new bearers of power – the feudal lords and the clergy – broke up the small-scale configuration of the Gothic town. The new palaces of war-enriched nobles, such as Generalissimo Albrecht von Valdštejn (Wallenstein), Václav Michna of Vacínov and Nostic, contrasted sharply with the dilapidation faced by the general public and absorbed a motley of old buildings, ruthlessly disrupting the scale of the town.

The clergy, on the other hand, with their long-ranging programmes, differed from these feudal overlords in the conception and realization of their ideas, which had sometimes originated even before the Battle of the White Mountain. Although the Jesuits managed to build only in the second half of the 17th century, their various disputes with the community concerning new boundaries, and the frequent mention of plans and alterations, are evidence of older conceptions that were the subject of continuous deliberation with their central authority in Rome. The Clementinum, the New Town College of St Ignatius, and the Lay House of St Nicholas in The Lesser Quarter were cornerstones of the city layout, while other orders, such as the Carmelite nuns, occupied large plots with gardens on the outskirts or at the city walls.

The Gothic fortifications were replaced by new Baroque ones with massive brick walls, and within them the city slowly recuperated after the Thirty Years War. Minor adaptations and restyling of houses made up the main activity. Families of north-Italian bricklayers, stonemasons and stucco workers who could not compete with first-class artists in their own country, moved into the city and brought local patterns and models from their north-Italian homes. As a result of this, the work produced in Prague became a mosaic of mutually unrelated and overlapping trends. Carlo Lurago (1615-84) from Valle Intelvi, was the outstanding artist of this period. His ability to organize, and his fine design, are especially evident in the Clementinum (1654-74), with its colossal order, where for the first time in Prague, a monumental motif which proportions and controls large blocks of building was used. This motif was modified several times later on, but this has not affected the north front of the Clementinum.

In the second half of the 17th century, after a period of economic depression, secular architecture once again began to make its mark on the cityscape. However, the city palaces of the aristocratic families of this era cannot compete with the Černín Palace, with its colossal order, towering over the west horizon of the city, indisputably an extraordinary structure. This praise is justified not only by the brilliant plans of the architect Francesco Caratti (†1677), which have been preserved, and by the high respect felt for his mastery by his contemporaries, but also by the remarkable Church of St Mary Magdalene – an interesting combination of centrally and axially planned construction.

Towards the end of the 17th century, what had amounted to an Italian monopoly over the building trade was beginning to be cracked by local artists and artisans – among them immigrants from southern Germany and Austria (Abraham Leuthner) and also from France (Jean-Baptiste Mathey, 1630-96). The work of the latter, as far as we know it today, was full of contradictions, but some of his buildings – such as the Church of St Francis of the Order of the Knights of the Cross (1679-88), built on the basis of a central plan, and the summer palace built for Count Václav Vojtěch of Šternberk in the outlying Prague district of Troja (1679-97) – belong to the best works of Prague Baroque, thanks to their clear and progressive plans, to their confident form and to their successful incorporation into the landscape and the panorama of the town.

Shortly before and just after 1700 we find a phenomenon which has not yet been fully investigated. The feudal system made it possible for people to amass large fortunes regardless of the extreme social contrasts, and thanks to the relative economic stability of the times an artistic movement of unusual creative force, daring ideas and captivating invention sprang up. This new artistic impulse exerted a strong influence at all strata of society, and stimulated the development of an authentic local Baroque style.

In architecture this caused a new evaluation of space and its articulation, of the incorporation of a structure into its urban surroundings; it produced a new organization of the plan, a tendency to shape matter dynamically (thus suggesting its dissolution), and a greater complexity of rhythmic schemes. It emphasized the optical aspect of the work, made use of a new morphology for binding/connecting elements and exploited illusions of space and perspective.

Over fifty years this movement remodelled the town, giving it an entirely new prospect. It established new landmarks and viewpoints; changed the entire aspect of the streets; conjured up many artistically impressive nooks, small squares, arcades and views; landscaped the city by incorporating terraced gardens into its overall design; and linked sculpture, painting and architecture into an indivisible whole. Guarino Guarini's plan for the Theatine Church of the Virgin of Etingen in The Lesser Quarter (1679) – although never realized – anticipates this period, and academic inquiry into the importance of this work for future developments has only just begun. However, it is beyond doubt that Prague provided fertile ground for the ideas of Domenico Martinelli (1650-1718), Johann Bernhard Fischer von Erlach (1656-1723), Johann Lucas von Hildebrandt (1668-1745), and above all for those of the Italians Guarino Guarini (1629-83) and Francesco Borromini (1599-1667).

However, the dispute concerning the authorship of the most expressive buildings of this High Baroque movement – the Church of St Nicholas in The Lesser Quarter and the Church of St Margaret in Břevnov – still continues. These works are closely connected with the names of Kryštof Dientzenhofer (1655-1722), Jan Blažej (Giovanni) Santini (1677-1723), Johann Lucas von Hildebrandt, and also to an unknown architect. The plans of both churches are based on interlocking ovals formed by complicated vaults; their façades are composed with the curve as the dominant characteristic of their plans; their structural composition derives its effect from an interplay between the beholder's field of vision, the rules of perspective, and their employment by sculptors and painters. According to the most recent study by M. Vilímková, it seems most likely that the design for the churches is to be attributed to Kryštof Dientzenhofer.

In palace architecture the plan also began to be differentiated. The massive cube was broken up, the vestibule and the staircase were set off as a ceremonial entrance space, often with an added forecourt or garden terrace. The piano nobile was enhanced by ornaments, and the front adorned by bases of variegated depth, cornices, sopraporte and portals.

A number of architects who worked in Prague (Marco Antonio Canevalle, 1652-1711; František Maximilián Kaňka, 1674-1766; Tomáš Haffenecker, 1669-1730; Giuseppe Bartolomeo Scotti, 1685-1737; Kristián Luna, 1671-1729; Giovanni Battista Alliprandi, 1667-1720; Pavel Ignác Bayer, 1656-1733), adapted and rebuilt old buildings in unprecedented numbers. But without doubt the culmination of this trend can be seen in the work of the ingenious Kilián Ignác Dientzenhofer (1689-1751), who was supremely adept at combining various influences. He gave the town new landmarks; his urban sensibility, the scope of his language of form, and his compositional invention are unparalleled.

By the second half of the 18th century, however, High Baroque had passed its peak (František Ignác Prée, 1702-55; Jan Josef Hrdlička, 1690-1771). Dramatic ideas of composition stagnated in the weak imitations of bourgeois façades and in Rococo ornamentation (architects Jan Josef Wirch, 1732-83; Josef Jäger, 1722-1793; Anselmo Martino Lurago, 1701-65). Building activity dwindled when the importance of Prague declined during the reign of Maria Theresa. Prague ended the 18th century in the calmness of a provincial town, with just a few classicist buildings.

Mass, Structure and Form

1. Plaster and Stucco

The stuccoed wall epitomizes Prague Baroque architecture in terms of the materials used, and as a visible expression of the spirit of the style. Plaster was used simply, with restraint but not without impact, to cover cracks in external walls. Thin layers of plaster cover quarried stonemasonry and mute the restlessness of its composition, while thick layers of plaster overlay both the interior and exterior of a building, sometimes polished to a mirror-like surface when the stucco lustro technique was employed. The quality of Prague lime and the skill of bricklayers and stucco workers – who knew how to shape complex systems of architectural, figured and floral decor in stucco, and how to give an illusion of large and organized natural formations – were prerequisites for the efforts of architects such as Kilián Ignác Dientzenhofer who created the body of their buildings by treating the curved façade and the wall, pillar and cornice details as if they had been moulded freehand in sculptor's clay.

Here we find the basis for the impact on the street created by Baroque houses and palaces, the façades of which shone with newly painted colourful nuances, alongside façades that had lost their glow with age or were even crumbling away. More than once, façades of a surprising asymmetry spring up – peculiar, vivid, deviating from the norm and striking because of their significantly changed proportions. Thick and thin layers of supplely moulded stucco formed original, innovative or conventional designs for main, side and garden façades. In Prague, however, we find a predominance of façades that were added to older, rebuilt and appropriately redecorated medieval houses. You can recognize these by their angular fronts and by the uneven distances of the bays and between window openings, for the irregularity of the original structure still governs the overlay of the new Baroque design executed in plaster and stucco. Stuccowork solved the problem of how to give form to the whole dazzling spectacle of Baroque design with its precisely composed scenery and its wealth of pilasters, lesenes, string courses, window aedicules, frames, sopraporte and parapets.

Stucco plaster asserts itself in the complicated and ostentatious draperies on palace and church façades, and in main reception rooms and ceremonial halls. But no less effective, and sometimes even more striking, are the characteristic qualities of stucco that come to light where it smooths the quiet flowing of walls in aisles, vestibules or side staircases with its endlessly white planes, undisturbed by relief; here, peace and strength may be emphasized by a modest decorative motif. Thus an aesthetic contrast is created between the simple, solid wall of the side face and the rich, sculpted main façade, and between the modest, compact garden wall and the sumptuousness of the vegetation it surrounds.

The Baroque period left to classicism an essentially more colourful city than is visible nowadays. The architects not only used stuccoes coloured by dye, but also painted stucco surfaces. Colour was an essential element of their stylistic conception and underwent changes as ideas altered. In the 17th century, tectonic devices were emphasized by cardinal red paint, or by mixing pulverized brick into the stucco. On the other hand, in the second half of the 18th century it was customary to achieve a 'reversed' effect by colouring the wall spaces and leaving the window frames and mouldings white. With the great masters of the Dientzenhofer family, and with Santini as well, we also find interiors in grey and white, and exteriors in natural colour or in strongly coloured lime stucco.

2. Stone

Stone and architecture – the words are almost synonyms, for stone is a symbol of the strength and durability of architecture. Thanks to stone's rich spectrum of colours and to its wide structural adaptability (which is revealed and accentuated by stonecutting) the tremendous supporting power and expressive charm of stone are found not only in the main architectural structure, but also in its small, functional and formal details. The granite used for the staircase leading to the entrances of the Church of St Nicholas in The Lesser Quarter, the sandstone of the grazing-stones in front of the Lobkovic Palace, or the flintstone pavement in the courtyard represent only some of the tones in the stone polyphony of Prague Baroque.

The leading voice is that of sandstone. Only the owners of the Slivenec marble quarries – the Order of the Knights of the Cross – could afford an extensive architectural composition in marble, as is evident in the interior of their Church of St Francis. This Mediterranean material – of splendid colour and finish when cut and polished – was the dream of Baroque architects working in Prague. But sandstone was by far the more easily available, and from it were hewn numerous portals, embrasures, pedestals, capitals, cornices, pylons, vases, balustrades, statues, pavings and steps.

The architects of the Baroque period related to solid, yet malleable, stone in a way that differs from how we view it today. Above all, stone – painted or covered with plaster – was a basic element of construction in walls. But stone offers other possibilities for expression. It has a granulated surface, and its crisp roughness, when used in interiors and in façades, creates an effective contrast with the soft and smooth whiteness of lime-based stucco. The forms brought out by the chisel of the sculptor or mason will never completely break free from the suggestion of weight and compact robustness, and these are the very qualities that contribute to monumental architecture. At the same time, the play of light and shadow on the rugged sandstone surface has a special aesthetic effect. Here, light does not flow smoothly and continuously over protrusions, nor does it hide in cavities, but twinkles and finely crumbles, as each grain of the mineral refracts a pointillist microvalue. The overall effect is that some forms are evoked as composed of sharp sparks, others of chiaroscuro semitones.

3. Brick

In the 17th and 18th centuries, building in Prague was also characterized by the use of unplastered brick wall. This is especially true of fortifications and for the walls supporting terrace gardens. This rough material, its regular structure having the effect of a geometrical net of joints, was used only sparsely for interiors. Instead of the ornamental patterns of Gothic or Renaissance brick walls, the simple stretching or heading bond prevails.

There were also differences in size: in contrast to the relatively constant size of large and heavy Gothic brick 'cakes', or the small bricks of the Renaissance period, architects used bricks of various sizes. The terraces of the Troja Palace were built of bricks much larger than those used for the interior walls of the Loreto shrine on the Hradčany. The brick walls are seldom monotonous – repairs in quarried stone or in bricks of a different size bring a welcome liveliness to the austere regularity of the bonds.

But bricks served more often as constructional material that remained hidden under the plaster. Kilián Ignác Dientzenhofer's vaults, thin shells of brick, would have been unthinkable without this material and without the outstanding skills of the bricklayers.

Pantiles of burnt brick clay cover town houses and palaces, almost without exception. They stand out especially in the intricate organism of The Lesser Quarter when viewed from the heights of Prague Castle or from Petřín Hill. This panorama offers a complex structure of striations in different directions. The way the tiles have been laid in the various segments, and the difference in heights between roofs, makes a patchwork of sharp-edged and round planes, creating a unique example of Baroque architectural 'design'.

4. Wood

The essential contribution of wood to the architecture of Prague, which was known from early medieval times as the 'city of stone', is evident in its enormous roof and ceiling structures. The functional value and aesthetic appeal of wood are revealed in beams and floorboards and in oak stairways, in front doors and in windows with shutters, and also – bearing in mind the total architectural effect of the fully furnished interior – in the furniture. This is true of the heavy, robust, solid furniture made for everyday use as well as well as the exquisite, refined pieces created to display the affluence of their owners.

The work of 17th and 18th century woodcarvers, cabinet-makers and carpenters, who knew how to make use of the material qualities of wood to create the most complicated forms of architectural and ornamental decoration, was closely linked to the activity of painters, gilders, blacksmiths and locksmiths. The cooperation between these crafts was of two sorts. On the one hand, oak front doors are decorated with other materials (such as painted or metalwork paterae, rosettes, tendrils and ornamental nails, or, on the inside, cast iron hinges and sliding bolts), and yet retain the full natural 'flavour' of wood, its peculiar dense firmness suggested by an expressive grain. The same effect was produced in splendid, costly tarsia doors of palaces, inlaid with various – occasionally imported – woods. Waxing gives depth to natural grains and original colours.

On the other hand, some methods of embellishment lent wood entirely new qualities, new functions and new roles, depending on whether it was inlaid, lacquered, painted in polychrome or gilded, or combined with stucco, metal or textiles. These techniques were especially employed in choir architecture. In the half-light of church interiors, black-painted wood takes on a sharp outline. The gilded, twisted columns, the cornice edges and the fine astragal mouldings, however, lose their definite contours – their glow in the semi-darkness dissolves their forms into elusive phantasms. Only from nearby does the structure of wood reveal itself, through fine cracks in the glossy, gilded surface.

54

Rhythm

When we walk through a city and move around the interiors of its buildings, we come to understand how a city and its structures grow out of the needs of its inhabitants, and how they correspond to the rhythm of life. The buildings themselves are firmly rooted in the ground, but the onlooker is driving, hurrying, walking past, or else pausing to look. Time, which defines the rhythm of movement of the spectator and, as such, constitutes a fourth dimension, naturally penetrates the relationships within architecture. The dimension of time is included as a compositional element in 17th and 18th century architectural design. The large compositions of countryside, parks and woods of this period were experienced to the rhythm of horse riding, interrupted by moments of repose and walking. One ascended festive staircases to the rhythm of a celebratory march; the garden as a decorative ornament is best perceived from the tranquility of a terrace behind a palace, or a balcony on a rear façade.

The rhythm, the repetition and alternation of elements or groups of elements plays an important part in the architectural design of each individual building. The buildings of the 17th and 18th centuries are too varied to assume a common principle underlying the rhythm of their compositions. However, the simplest of rhythms – plain repetition – is present in all buildings. Everyone is familiar with the rhythm of stairs, an example of a monotonously repeated element. Baroque art greatly favoured this rhythmic motif, and architects did not shy from going to extremes, employing it for long staircases that lead to the summits of places of pilgrimage, and also for garden stairs – such as those that surmount the slopes of Petřín Hill or of Prague Castle. Staircases show the interplay between rhythmical abstraction and the concreteness of sandstone, between precision and the elegance of articulated mass.

The effect of the seemingly endless repetition of the huge beams of rough, natural-looking wood that span the large distance between the supports in the ceiling of the Riding School in Prague (architect Mathey), is of a similar nature. Analogous examples are to be seen in the regular rhythm of vaults (e.g. nave and choir of StJacob's), in balusters (e.g. the loggia of the Valdštejn Palace), in arcades (e.g. the houses on Pohořelec Square), and – on a different level – in the paving and benches of churches (e.g. St Nicholas').

In addition to these timeless, universal architectural motifs, architects of the 17th and 18th centuries used an unusually wide range of rhythmical devices. Architectural design of this period was, therefore, more complicated than it had been in the two preceding centuries. The architect did not work with only one motif, repeating it as an entity or as a group, but superimposed motifs that developed in horizontal, vertical and diagonal directions, giving the design an organic quality. Tectonic systems, their refractions and multiplications as well as the suggestion of various spatial planes, intertwine in the rhythm, like melodies running through each other. The most common example is that of a wall having a frames of lesenes and compounds of superimposed pilasters on pedestals. These systems of projecting and receding forms, and the multiplication and interpenetration of motifs, often brought about nearly insoluble problems with regard to details.

The spectator often cannot grasp the composition as a whole, and has to analyse it into its basic schemes. However, different angles of view enable him to recognize rhythmical motifs either in a simplified and abstracted fragment or, conversely, as an impenetrable, accumulated mass of 'rhymed rhythms'. Both ways of perceiving have to be taken seriously in 18th century architecture. Such angles of view were a source of inspiration not only for the fresco painters of the period, who loved the illusions of perspective and foreshortened perspective, but also for other artists and sculptors of the time. Baroque architecture, like Baroque music, is in its complicated rhythmical manifestations a suspension of mutually dependent and independent groupings and arrangements. As the music theorist Hutter puts it: 'The complexity and the confusion of the fabric as a whole do not distort individual voices. On the contrary, each voice is equipped with an artistic organism that is endowed with a life of its own, so that it stays alive when it is passed on to others.'

The rhythm of the Černín Palace façade, of the pilasters of the loggia, or of the details of the pedestals of the front façade of the Church of St Salvator, of the rear façade of the Church of St Bartholomew, of the façade of the Clementinum in the Knights of the Cross Street, of the Cross and of the walls of the nave of the Church of St Nicholas – each of these is derived from a quite different conception. In the Černín Palace, for example, the motif of each bay alternating with triangular and segmental window pediments is repeated almost endlessly, and by means of perspective is simplified to a rhythm of columns. But in the case of the Clementinum, the nervous character of the projecting and receding parts is highlighted by multiplication and foreshortened perspective. The façade is ruled by a far more complicated system, which cannot be attained with the help of a pilaster order.

The principle of addition and multiplication of motifs is in sharp contrast with the principle which isolates parts from the whole. The north side of the Church of St Bartholomew (Kilián Ignác Dientzenhofer) is ruled by a rhythm as complex and well thought-out as in the examples mentioned above. Motifs are arranged not only horizontally and vertically, but also diagonally – thus creating internal rhythmical relations, individually, in clusters, or penetrating each other. The motifs do not cross the boundaries of the squares of the basic modular grid, but time and again return to their axes and centres. This work belongs to the most sophisticated rhythmical projects of Prague architecture.

The nave of the Church of St Nicholas and its system of vaults present an even more complicated design. As in Bach's fugues, one motif does not follow the other in strict succession, but already appears before the preceding one has died away, thus creating an overlapping motif. The cylindrical spaces forming the nave intersect, only parts of its walls remain, and the vault is broken up by invading new themes. This admirable architectural composition is generated by a certain impatience, by the acceleration of tempo and the absorption of one group by the next even before its form has faded. These often dazzling rhythmical variations are the culmination, but also the finale of 18th century architecture.

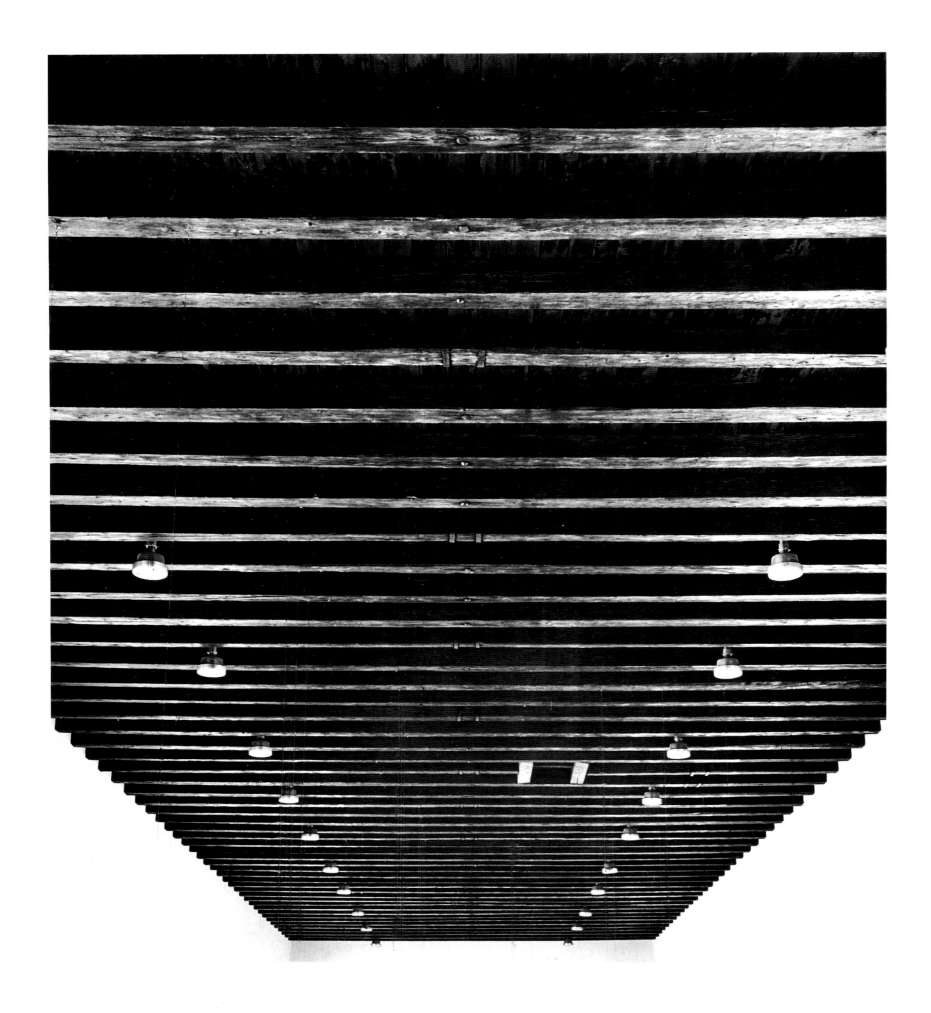

Tectonics

Extensive contact between Bohemia and the regions of classical antiquity had, as early as the Romanesque and Gothic periods, resulted in a steady absorption of ancient architectural forms. The Renaissance did not introduce new elements, but a new way of organizing them. Theoretical knowledge of the architectural elements of the Tuscan, Ionic, Corinthian or Composite orders became more and more refined, so that by 1700 a perfect system of architectural orders could be formulated.

The architects in Prague, who had sometimes even studied at universities and were thoroughly familiar with contemporary European developments, were experts on classical and Renaissance orders. Since the publishing of theoretical works and pattern books by Palladio, Serlio, Scamozzi and Vignola, right up to the *Theatrum architecturae civilis* (published by Leonardus Dientzenhofer in 1697), it had become possible to compare orders and authorities. A perfect knowledge of the various possibilities of the employment of orders and their proportions, and of modules and rhythmic qualities, was typical of the leading architects, especially of the two Dientzenhofers.

The architecture of the early 18th century was not based on ignorance or distortion of the orders, but, on the contrary, on a perfect knowledge of their numerous possibilities and variants. The study of sample and pattern books shows us that Renaissance theoretical works by Alberti and Serlio already contain seeds of designs that later came to be called Baroque. Broken entablatures, splayed soffits, alternating triangular and segmental pediments, an increase in the number of pillars, broken pediments, the smoothly curved transition of the cornice into the pediment, a predilection for superimposed pillars, the employment of the colossal order and the combination of orders in differing dimensions – all this was already known to Renaissance architects of the 16th and often even of the 15th century. Drawings handed down to us by Renaissance theoreticians, and the creativity of Hellenistic classical architecture, show the complex roots of High Baroque forms and tectonics and the numerous possibilities inherent in such a seemingly unalterable and standardized tectonic system.

The works of the foremost Prague architects show a range of forms varying from the simplicity of the wall, to the tectonic expression of active and passive structural elements that have been carried through with such consistency that it is difficult to find a parallel even in modern architecture. Analysis of plans and volumes shows that they even succeeded in finding a way of integrating Gothic skeletons with classical and Renaissance forms. Thus the remarkable unity of vault systems and superimposed pillar groups could be achieved possibly only in Prague, at this junction of cultures, of northern and southern trends of thought.

First and foremost, it is worth noticing how wall tectonics finds artistic expression. Naturalistic elements penetrate the architecture, and walls are shaped like rocks or rock formations. The abyss into which the giants on the staircase in Troja fall, or the chapel in the garden of the Carmelite nuns at the Church of St Joseph in The Lesser Quarter – all this is artificial nature. Similarly, artificial rock makes up the bases of statues on Charles Bridge. The extremely popular motif of lava-like, stalactite walls reached fantastic proportions in the garden walls of the Valdštejn Palace. These motifs naturalistically accentuate the structural composition of the walls.

Kilián Ignác Dientzenhofer chose a different way to accentuate the structural composition of a wall. The garden wall of the villa that he designed for his brother has an air of desolation, as if the ravages of time had left their mark in architectural miniature. However, it is actually a remarkable example of creative use of a Romanesque motif.

Architects used plastered brick as a sculptural medium, as pliable mass. This is how Kryštof Dientzenhofer built the Church of St Margaret in Břevnov and how Kilián Ignác Dientzenhofer constructed the outer wall, like an enveloping mantle, of the Church of St John Nepomuk on the Rocks, the garden front of his villa in Smíchov and the façade of the Church of St Thomas in The Lesser Quarter. This emphasis on the plasticity of mass contrasts with the large façade organized according to an architectural order system consisting of supported and supporting parts, of active and passive elements.

Although tectonic order systems have acquired a symbolic value, their gradual refinement of form remained unquestioned. Plinths, pedestals, column shafts, capitals, architraves and cornices became independent elements of expression, monuments in themselves. What subtlety, feeling for material and compositional intricacy is found in the base of the Thun Palace on Neruda Street! The rustication motif is carried through rigorously. The noticeably set-forward facets of the blocks of the ashlar, their sharply inclined chamfers, the gently protruding edges and the vibrantly chiselled sandstone surface – are all witnesses to the experienced hand of the architect and mason. The light finely moulds itself to the facets and chamfers of the ashlar walls, turned to us and away from us. The full-frontal view enables us to admire the balanced proportions and the intricate rhythms of the surfaces.

A beautiful example of base design, founded on projecting and recessed bands, was created by Kryštof Dientzenhofer on the exterior of the nave of the Church of St Nicholas in The Lesser Quarter. Because of their elemental form, the projecting columns achieve their own, independent plastic qualities. In 18th century paintings, for example, columns were favoured not only as embellishment, but also as objects that lent prestige and dignity, and created new compositional relations.

If we look at the columns set into in the lower part of the pillars of the portal of the Valdštejn Palace in The Lesser Quarter, we get the impression that they go beyond being a constructional element within the tectonic design. On closer inspection, the cylindrical column shaft with entasis, inserted into the pillar niche, gains autonomy. All forms are reduced to fundamental stereometric volumes – cylinder, torus, block – which are artistically related to each other. Whereas the vertical cylinder of the column has been hewn with great care, the rusticated pillar stands in stark contrast with its coarse surface, accentuated by horizontal joints. The active and refined constructional element – the shaft with entasis – is monolithic; the pillar is rusticated and, by its coarseness, brought closer to the original unhewn material.

The plastered Tuscan coupled columns of the loggia of the Valdštejn Palace have a lightness and elegance that belie their large dimensions. Only on closer consideration does the spectator realize just how weighty they are. Centuries of development, and the accumulated knowledge of generations, have contributed to a nobility of form of the individual elements, and to the cultivation of proportion, contour and tectonic composition.

The base of the Clementinum, which we easily pass by without noticing, stands alone, tranquil and monumental; it expresses the serenity and venerability of architecture. The strict restraint of vertical and horizontal parts, of perpendicular groups of projecting and recessed parts, bands and planes, together with the granulated sandstone and lively chiselled surfaces, are something more than just an example of a particular tectonic system.

As a result of the projections, superimposed pillars and diagonally arranged designs, the capitals, broken architraves and cornices often ended up in isolated positions, which, incidentally, enhances their individual effect.
Indeed, cornices became the most formative motif in High Baroque building. Around 1700 a remarkable break occurred in the way these components were conceived. Theoretical books of patterns and examples provided a variety of sets of rules of composition and of mutual proportions of parts for even the most complicated and strictly formal of order systems. Up to the time of Mathey, the ability of the architect who designed and supervised a project could be judged from the degree of perfection with which he applied these theoretical models. In the period following the works of Santini, Kryštof Dientzenhofer and others, the attitude of architects towards traditional profiling and the plastic use of building components suddenly changed, and began to show a strong individualizing emphasis on the constituent elements. Today, we know that in classical systems, particularly those of Asia Minor and of the late Hellenistic phase, a similar individualising trend existed. Drawings by Michelangelo, in which he approaches architectural components in an almost sculptural way, prove that there were possibilities latent within the order systems of classical antiquity that could later be given expression by his genius. It is as yet not quite clear what made Borromini and Guarini exploit this part of the classical language of forms; it is not even known whether they had any knowledge of it, while the relationship between architects working in Bohemia and Prague and these great Italian artists is clouded by obscurity and mystery. Nevertheless, the existing works are evidence of creative connections between Prague and Bohemia on the one hand and, on the other, the compositions of Borromini and Guarini and, in a wider sense, the conceptions of Michelangelo and of Hellenistic antiquity as well.

The penetration of the curve into the plan of a building and the use of a system of interlocking floor plans increased the importance of cornices and cornice sections. These allow us to trace the compositional intentions of the designer, which could otherwise be discerned only with difficulty. After 1700, as if carried on the wings of fantasy, architects in Prague modelled cornices ranging from sharp, superimposed formations that gave architectural expression to a certain nervousness by their extruding and receding planes, cymae and cornices, to freely flowing waves and overhangs with soft outlines. Thus extraordinarily powerful profiles often project from the walls, penetrating into space like sculpted forms. Though the cornice was designed in frontal elevation, this design practice included the accumulated experience of many years, in the effects and changes brought about by foreshortened perspective and by the rules of perspective. It is in the foreshortened perspective, in particular, that each supporting or projecting element is highlighted. Light accentuates the plasticity and substance of its form; shadow multiplies the many refractions, or the flowing movement of the soft curves moulded in stucco.

Especially in the work of the greatest master of Prague architecture, Kilián Ignác Dientzenhofer, an in-depth study of this profiling, and of the relation between supporting and connecting components, and between planes and cornices, reveals that the traditional relationship between supporting and supported element is retained. This is in spite of the freedom reigning in the softened outlines of planes, in the individualization of components through deep undercuts and joints, and in the divisions into new rhythmic groups and subgroups. Even the details convince us time and again of the confident control and deep knowledge of this architect, who knew how to utilize his artistic sovereignty to achieve new artistic goals. His cornices can be compared with musical compositions. They reflect a similar enchantment of the senses by form as is to be found on a different level in sculpture, music and painting, and in all those works that express most profoundly the genius loci of Bohemia.

The Baroque architecture of Prague again and again confirms that the mere study of order systems taken as morphological formulae is inadequate. Reality always went beyond this boundary. The accumulation of tectonic systems was combined with a sculptural conception of building material. This becomes apparent in the plans of pillar groups from which the order was to be realized, which became more and more irregular and intricate.

Closer observation of separate plans reveals the handwriting of individual architects for here they had already laid down the principles of the over-all composition of the building to be constructed and, in the case of the more complicated compositions, their deep inner coherence is already manifest.

By activating the load-bearing parts (the pillars) and by preserving the unarticulated, non-loadbearing walls between the pillars, the architect came so near to the Gothic system that, at this level, a close relationship between Gothic and Baroque exists. The pilaster no longer appears as an individual element, but as an inseparable part of the whole pilaster group, in which individual members are slid behind each other. This can be seen only partly, but we sense all the more intensely that we do not encounter here a mere profiling of the surface of a cubic mass, but a multiplication of tectonic activity. As in High Gothic construction, the consistency of the tectonic system meant that the base also determined the system directly below the vaulting, i.e. the system of cornices. The inner logic of this system is also closely linked with that of Gothic.

It is true that the Gothic-styled Baroque fantasies of Santini are not a speciality of Prague, but the vaulting systems of the Church of St Nicholas in The Lesser Quarter, and the freely formed profiles of its portal and window soffits are telling evidence of a closely related conception of modelling and of plasticity of mass.

The sum of collected knowledge of the precedence of orders and tectonic systems is represented by the tower of the Church of St Nicholas. The symbolic mastering of the weight of the structure is expressed by differing orders employed on different levels, from the Attic-Ionic to a free paraphrase of the Composite order. The architect strengthens pillars arranged on the diagonal by groups of pilasters, antae and half-columns, and employs intentional illusions of perspective and a subtle transformation in the plans. The tower – late Renaissance and Mannerist architectural pattern books reveal a predilection for solving this problem – became, in the interpretation of Kilián Ignác Dientzenhofer, a great individual work of art. In the same manner in which he involved older urban concepts when placing the tower within the framework of a block, he also seeks contact with the formal systems of older pattern books. But, thanks to his gifts, he created a work which triumphantly dominates the panorama of The Lesser Quarter.

Light and Shades

The change in effect caused by the movement of light was one of the main dynamic components of Baroque architecture. A beam of light glancing from detail to detail, would distinguish and continuously establish new relationships between them. But the angle and movement of the sun result in a cyclical repetition of this single experience. The sun's rays transform three-dimensional objects by lighting parts that were once plunged into shadow and vice versa. Light 'breathes life' into the inanimate architectural mass and its tectonic compound. The artistic effect is brought out in a whole gamut of chiaroscuro tensions, ranging from sharp contrasts to a calm, 'lightless' middle ground. If one seeks to understand architecture, these effects cannot be ignored. Works of architecture cannot be studied in isolation, but should be understood in close connection with the environment and atmospheric changes. Even natural extremes of light enrich our perception of architectural compositions and bring out unsuspected (but nonetheless real) transformations. The material essence doesn't change, it is our perception that lies at the base of these transformations.

The base of Černín Palace on Hradčany, with its expressive rustication and its sharply chiselled masonry, provides – when looked at from the front and lit by diffused light – a completely different experience than when hit by light rays at an angle of 45 degrees. Then, suddenly, the powerful rhythm of the projecting column pedestals stands out as the leading compositional theme. Under similar light conditions, the rustication reflects different amounts of light towards the various parts of the façade. If we look into the reason for this, we find that the environment plays an important role in the lighting. As we follow the façade, the situation gradually changes. Different effects occur, determined by the different colours of the marble mosaic pavement, by the projecting presence of the balcony (or by its absence), and by the surrounding lawns or paving.

As time passes, light continuously creates new groupings of forms. Observe the change from the lit to the unlit appearance of a building or part of a building, and you will notice many fine and powerful artistic effects. The architects of the High Baroque employed a wide scale of differing light effects in their compositions. Effects ranged from the strictly linear – sharp-edged layers of pilaster prisms or cornice sections – to the soft (rounded and elongated cylinders, undulations, curved surfaces of walls, roofs, and belfries, as well as details as cones, as the cylindrical shafts of columns, echini, cymae, etc.).

In the 18th century the scope of these effects was considerably increased because in the designs of this period horizontal sections through a building differed in their outlines at different heights. Light enhances the effect of countermovement suggested by these differing outlines as it picks out curved planes that form a transition from the lower-floor outline to the higher one, traced by the cornice above the windows at each level. Free sculpted formations projecting from the walls subtly temper the light, toning it down to half-light and shade. Whether in diffused or direct light, the building is full of restlessness. Luminous accents and curves grow out of shade. The edge of a cornice, a pilaster or pillar suddenly interrupts the play of light.

The fronts of Baroque buildings, photographed when the sun illuminates them with glaring sidelight, seem to gain solidity. In contrast, frontal lighting strikes shadows that seem to break up the façade into highlighted parts. This emphasizes the rhythm of the composition, the dramatic organization and the angularity of the ordering system – yet the building seems to loose solidity.

Diffused lighting has a sensual effect on form. In the interiors of their most impressive works, Kryštof and Kilián Ignác Dientzenhofer made use of hidden light sources by lighting the main space from adjoining ones which received direct daylight. Light is reflected and refracted, and floods the body of the building in such a way that its origins and its direction are difficult to trace. The interior is suffused with light and permeated by a quiet glow. This is the effect created in the adjoining north rooms, staircases, galleries, and also in the main nave of the Church of St Nicholas in The Lesser Quarter. The younger Dientzenhofer went even further, and with the help of illusions of perspective, mirrors and cunningly positioned flat surfaces, guided daylight entering the tall, narrow side-windows to a wing that stands out particularly within the theatre-like scene of the altar in the apse. In doing so he overcame all difficulties caused by creating an indirect route for the light, although a simpler, direct solution to the problem would have been possible.

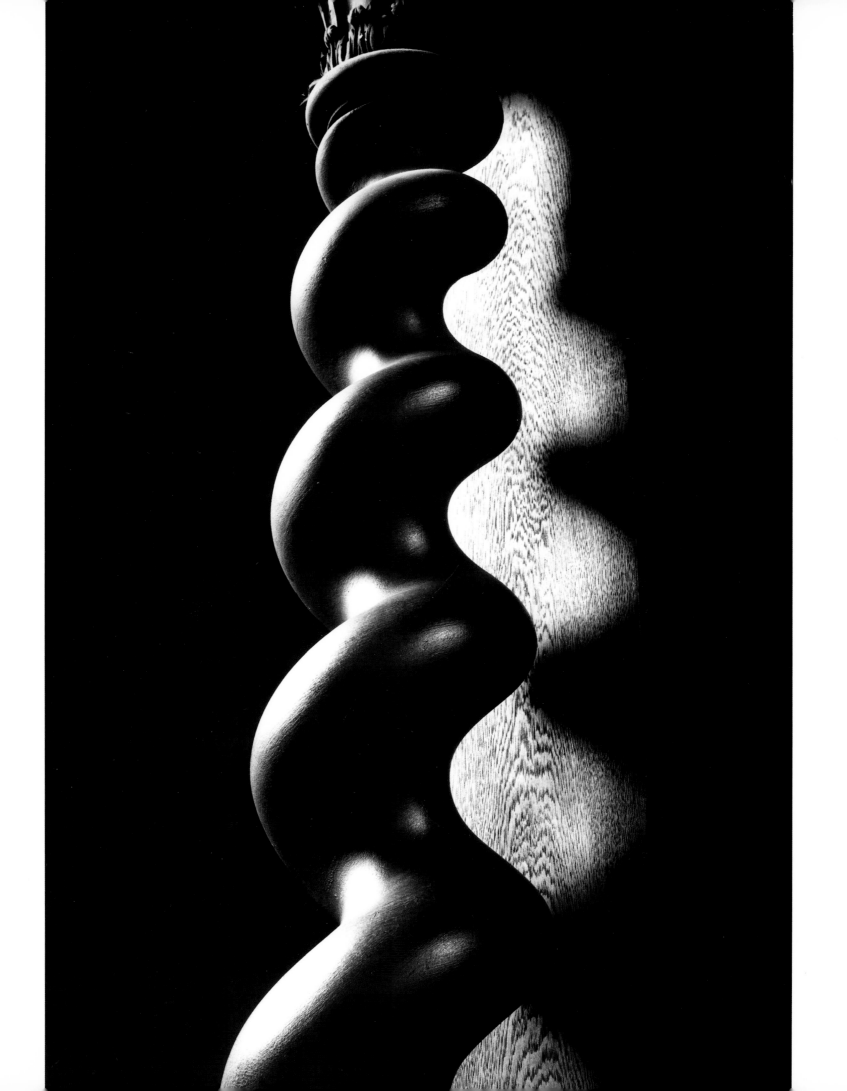

Ornament

Ultimately, it was painting, sculpture and other art forms that gave Baroque interiors and exteriors their distinctive appearance. However, the mixture of ugliness and beauty, of extravagance of form and asceticism, characteristic of art of the 17th and 18th century was, perhaps, only to be understood again in the works of the Expressionist artists and architects of the 20th century.

As to the craft of their work, not only architects, but also sculptors, painters, decorators, cabinet-makers, stonemasons and stucco workers had at their disposal a large number of model and pattern source books containing numerous basic models for variation and modification. Some motifs became the expressions of characteristic trends that demarcate certain periods. In the 17th century, Dutch and German decorative systems, with their typical worked metal motifs and scrollwork, made an impression. The middle of the 17th century is characterized by high stucco relief; naturalistic fruit garlands and scallop infills. Towards the end of the century, the acanthus leaf – richly developed with ribbons and flowers – became popular. Later this was replaced by delicately moulded surface ornament with latticework motifs, which, in the second half of the 18th century, gave way to rocaille decoration. Towards the end of the century a certain calming down occurs with the arrival of classicism, with its predilection for ornamental motifs inspired by ancient Greek and Roman designs.

Yet these characteristic designs are but exterior manifestations of a period which was many-facetted and full of contradictions, in life as in art. The asceticism of spirit and form of the Lay House in The Lesser Quarter, recommended by the General of the Jesuit order to the Superior and its builder, is in sharp contrast to the rich architecture of the Church of St Nicholas, which immediately adjoins it.

Ornamentation most durably fulfilled the need to make sensual conceptions tangible. Painters, sculptors and stucco workers helped to transpose abstract images into concrete forms. In illusionary perspective, the frescoes, stuccowork and statues brought the entire transcendental world closer to the human scale and made it more understandable. These illusions were created with the quiet consent of the spectator, like a game with rules tacitly agreed upon, for all illusions of perspective become 'absurd' if the viewer moves away from the presupposed vanishing point or viewing axis.

The mixture of rational and absurd elements escorts us on each step through a room, and accompanies us in the vicinity of a wall, where painted or stucco decoration is executed in an illusive way. The mutual reciprocity between the elements is apparent, and surprises us with its consistency and naturalness – both in large fresco conceptions and in the morphological and tectonic details of joints, consoles, sunk crossbeams and door soffits, all of which have been altered by the rules of illusory perspective. Decorative views of ideal landscapes and illusory architectural spaces enhance the impression of grandeur, even audacity. Interiors change into grottoes; décor grows alarmingly rank in the stalactite-like formations of the vaulting of the Valdštejn Palace.

In stark contrast to the interiors oversaturated by decoration, or the lava-like garden walls of the Valdštejn Palace, are the naive, charming, softly coloured façades of the small houses, with their stucco decorations, stone tablets, and the ornamental infills of their portals and doors. These guide us into a world of earthly scale, of worry and poverty; they reflect the soul of the unknown craftsman and artist. The door of the portal of the Convent of St Thomas speaks a simple language – the symbolic and artistic forms of pain and spiritual tranquility are easily intelligible.

There is yet another ornamental motif which permeated the whole of the 17th and 18th centuries: the use of tectonic systems as wall decoration. It is difficult to determine where architectural compositions lose their tectonic importance and become decorative. All walls of the interior of the Valdštejn loggia are articulated by complicated tectonics. This rhythmic and well-formed articulation of the walls facilitates orientation in such a gigantic space.

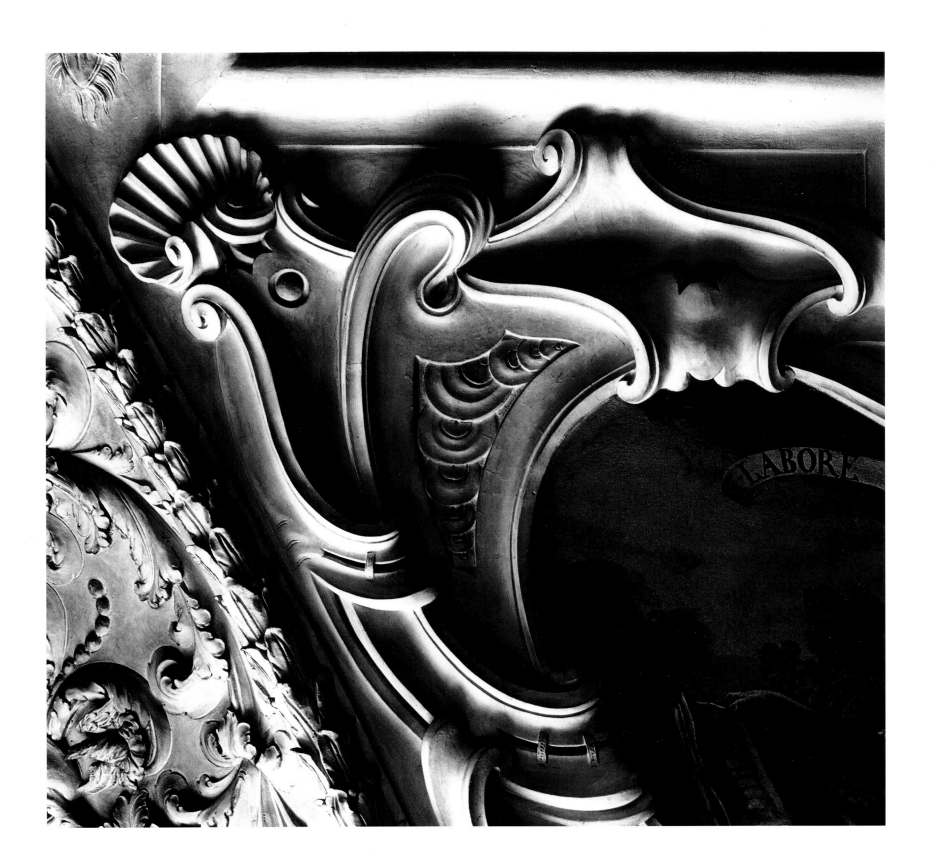

The Curve in Plan and Space:
The Countermovement of Matter

After 1700 the curved line, so characteristic of Prague Baroque architecture, appeared in the plans of buildings as the expression of the incessant striving for a supremely plastic and dynamic architecture. The transfer of plasticity from elevation to plan released hitherto unthought-of possibilities of composition. Furthermore, knowledge of perspective developed to extremes influenced the work of architects decisively.

Why is it that the High Baroque composition ideas of Borromini and Guarini, derived from the properties of curves, found such response in Prague? We are rightly reminded here of the complicated vaulting and curves of Vladislav Hall. More than once Romanesque and Gothic buildings were repacked in a Renaissance or a Baroque 'shell'. The late-Gothic art of vaulting was overlaid by imported Renaissance styles, and the art of curved plan and space was forgotten for almost two centuries. Renaissance and 17th century architecture brought out the curve mainly in the elevation of semicircular faces of lunettes, in the archivolts of arcades, in arched windows and curved gables. In the plan, only the circle remained as the expression of the endeavour for greater compactness in centrally planned buildings.

The transfer into the plan of the complicated curve as a means of expression (at the turn of the 17th and 18th centuries), not only presented the architects with problems that had already been encountered in the late-Gothic period, but also with entirely new ones. Thanks to the work of Borromini and Guarini, the plan of a building began to hold far greater significance. Architects found that plasticity could be achieved far more easily by a curved plan than by accumulating volume in a façade that was basically flat. In Bohemia this understanding was facilitated by gifted artists, who eminently realized these architectural ideas. Prague became the leading centre of architectural innovation of the period. The curve appeared not only in the architectural plans of palaces and churches, but pervaded the building as a whole, even in apparently unalterably rigid systems. Whereas the modules of order systems in elevations did not change, in the plan even the component parts developed to a high degree of complexity. Here, pedestals, plinths and abaci were bent together with architraves and cornices.

The curve was not confined to the plan, but pervaded the whole organism of the building. Curved motifs are found in the patterns of paving stones. Curved steps in grand staircases invoke a countermovement of volume, and the curves of barrel vaults approach each other from many different angles, then move apart again. Snakelike balustrades wind along the perimeter of daringly cut-out organ lofts, or along palace balconies (e.g. the balcony on the front of the Černín palace). The curve also became a basic component of the layout of gardens and terraces. As a result of these complicated curved plans, construction became increasingly difficult, especially in vaulting technique which began to display unparalleled bravura. Cabinets, benches, picture frames, organ cases, but also garden walls were no longer set in a flat plane, but – thanks to an intricately curved plan – became multi-dimensional, with several planes of depth.

Sketches preserved from the period enable us to learn the working procedure of an architect. We see how the fundamental idea is transferred from the whole to the detailed, and how the original form is projected into both an overall spatial concept and into the formation of detail. Artistic craft and decoration go back to the same sources as architecture.

Not only the main spaces, but also even quite unimportant rooms are planned in the same way. Our respect for the creators of these stylistically unified compositions grows with our knowledge of these secondary spaces. In the Church of St Nicholas in The Lesser Quarter we find such examples in the side staircases, in the side passages behind the galleries, in the inaccessible side chapels at the entrance of the church and also in the basement. We can even say that, for example, in the wall that separates the side apse from the gallery on the first floor, the same architectural struggle with volume is fought out as in the church façade, but on a simpler level. The convex surface swells slightly towards the viewer, while its further penetration of the side walls and barrel vault creates a sharp edge, which is at first linear and then becomes curved. A window, broken asymmetrically into the wall, provides the connecting link between the spaces and offers a view into the world of decoration, statues and frescoes at the entrance side of the church. The soft play of rounded surfaces, curves and solid volumes is bathed in diffuse light, which shapes them and brings them to life. The refined and the bulky (which is masked by the simplest of means) create a fantastic combination of curves, volumes and wall surfaces. These melt with the openings into numerous secondary rooms and to the side areas in front of the entrance to the inner spiral staircase. Thus the main and secondary parts of the building achieve a unity of expression.

It is typical of the High Baroque architecture of Prague that the elevation of a building does not change as radically as the plan. Though the elevation is enriched by curves both in silhouette and in individual details of cornices, window openings and portals, the main contribution lies elsewhere. By combining curvature in the elevation and in the plan, the architect succeeds in strengthening the effect of entire formations, especially of cornices when seen in foreshortened perspective. These change in an extraordinarily complex manner into fantastic shapes that remind us of the surge of a windswept sea. The architect combines this surprising layering and countermovement of matter with the accumulation and mixing of shapes and curves. The direction of the fantastically curved structures changes from horizontal to vertical. The piling up and even crowding together of volumes, their violent tearing apart and rejoining, are all the direct results of the penetration of the curve into the plan of a building. Like the great 17th century mathematician Leibnitz, the creators of these architectural compositions reckoned with a state of rest that is inseparably linked with movement.

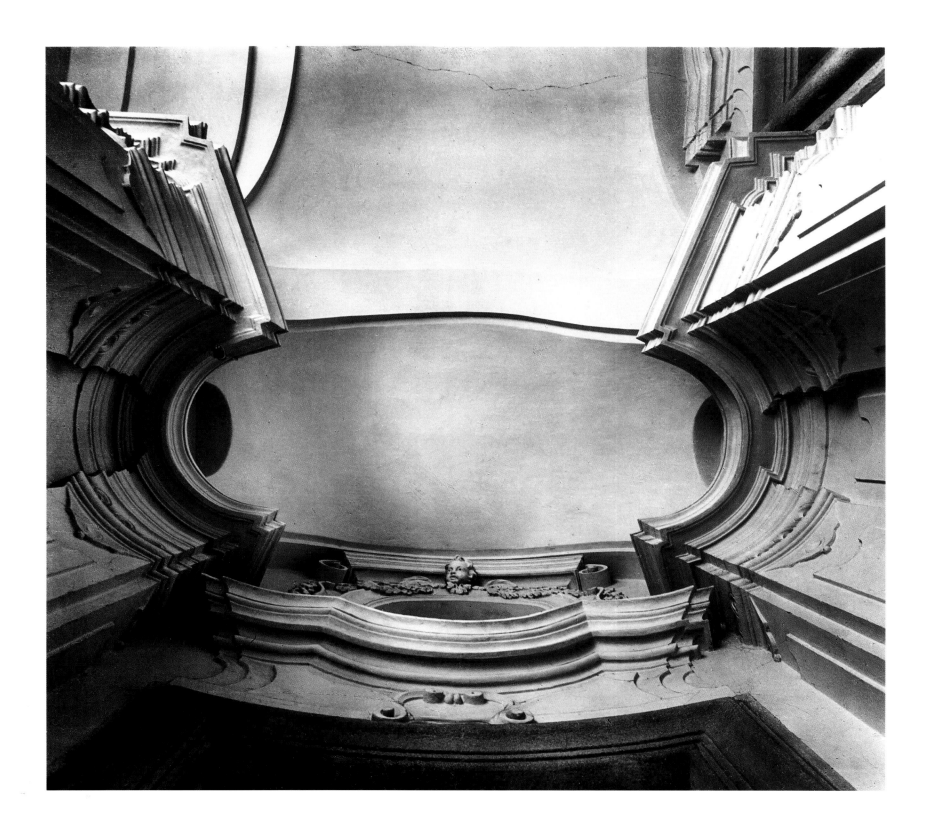

Contrast and Unity

Attempts to explain the stylistic characteristics of art of the 17th and 18th centuries are at loggerheads with each other when it comes to the principles of Baroque aesthetics. It is apparent, over and over again, that not only within the separate artistic fields, but also within brief periods of time, the work of important architects and even single buildings contain opposing tendencies. Sometimes the architect was forced to give up his original intentions – either under pressure from a new or deviant aesthetic inherent in a building constructed by a foreign predecessor, or in order to comply with the builder's wishes. Large Baroque constructions may be surprisingly complicated, and their 'stylistic disharmony' may act as a source of inspiration to today's artistic and architectural sensibilities. The twofold Baroque theme of contrast and unity can be traced in each individual building.

That two worlds of opposing architectural intentions can be created alongside each other, is shown by the Lay House and the Church of St Nicholas in The Lesser Quarter of Prague. The fantastic play of forms, volumes and undulating masses, as well as of light effects expressing complicated morphological thinking, that is achieved in the church façade, is directly connected to an austere and disciplined building that refuses the participation of the beholder, and that was meant to embody the strength of doctrine of the Society of Jesus. The client – who commissioned the architect to design a college building that would persuade the beholder of the order's dedication to the vow of poverty – completely changed his intentions when it came to the construction of the church. The immense scale of both buildings is all the more marked in the one where the absolute lack of ornament seems almost presumptuous; its humility inspires trust, and its simplicity of form conveys most penetratingly the purposeful asceticism of the Jesuits.

In striking contrast with the 'machinelike' rhythm, the absolute lack of ornament and the effects of light on the front of the Lay House, is the façade of the Church of St Nicholas. The latter building welcomes the passer-by with open arms, and its appearance gave Prague a new landmark. The façade only hints at the nature of the interior, as it is a fundamentally independent composition. The symmetrical division into a nave with side-aisles is reflected in the proportions of the façade divisions and the placement of windows. The expressive motif of the façade – its undulating outer wall – is unique, and contrasts sharply with the central part of the inner wall covering the nave and the organ loft, which is flat. Because of their curved plans, both side chapels would appear to require a deviation of the concave outer wall. In reality, however, the convex surface of their interiors, and the concave surface of the exterior are executed in antithesis to each other. Thus, in the main outlines we find a dualism of inner and outer composition. The complex curve is there to be perceived by the spectator and does not permeate the entire mass of the wall.

On this massive body the architect has made use of the fine fabric of a strictly tectonic pilaster system. The extraordinarily rare ways in which light is exploited enable us to follow the transition of vertical forces from the pilasters into parts of the architraves and cornices, and into the pilaster order of the first floor. But even the accentuated cornice bonds on the first floor (which constitute the main cornice) do not conclude the movement of the vertical tectonic forces. The movement continues on both sides above the pilasters of the gable to the final outline. This vertical thrust is attacked and constricted by the horizontal elements of the pedestals, architraves, friezes and binding parts. This gives the front subtlety and virtuosity. Next to the overwhelming, countermoving masses, there is the continuously pulsating, peaceful life of tectonic forces which coerces them into disciplined formations. This contrast between powerful masses and the fine, austere and almost mathematically perfect counterpoint is characteristic of Baroque music as well. During the course of less than a quarter of a century, the ideas of one and the same client – the Jesuits – and of the architect have changed completely, to the point of antithesis.

Perhaps a less noticeable (but more fundamental) difference in the conception of the relation between the plan and the edifice which grows out of it, is provided by a comparison of two conceptually contrasting tendencies – the classic and the dynamic. Two of the many possible examples of this are the courtyard of the Lobkovic Palace and the interior of the Church of St Joseph in The Lesser Quarter. Although both buildings were erected shortly after each other, their architects started from completely different conceptions.

The wide-angle view into the interior of the Church of St Joseph reveals a highly cultivated environment, one in which classicism is still very much a source of architectural inspiration. Although it was necessary to squeeze the originally circular plan of the central space of the nave into a narrow site, disrupting the peace and balance of the space in all its directions and dimensions, the column shafts are still bathed in the diffused light from the dome lantern, which creates an academically balanced and serene enclosed space. This Viennese or Italian conception of space, however, was composed and altered by local artists in all its details, from the marble paving, the carved oak benches and the altar paintings to the cabinet work. The original academic conception, which originated outside the Czech environment, was restrained both by this environment and by the specific conditions of the site, and yet remain identifiable in the building.

On the other hand, the garden courtyard of the Lobkovic Palace displays a beautifully articulated plan, where the façade and the garden wall stand in perfect contrapuntal relationship with each other. The architect achieved a passionate countermotion of building volumes, which strive against each other in violent waves. Towards the garden, these breakers overflow the fence with its ornamental vases which help to shape the complicated space of the courtyard, in which the curves of the plan and countermotion of mass have become the leading compositional principle. It is a world of tension and high agitation, a world of academic conceptions concerning the role of the wall in architecture (take, for example, the interior of the Church of St Joseph), a world unsettled by the stream of dynamic architecture.

Prague offers numerous examples of the symbiosis of differing compositional systems within one building. Kilián Ignác Dientzenhofer incorporated an older Gothic tower into the complicated façade of the Church of St Thomas. The simple rectangular form of the tower is firmly anchored in the wavy façade, which is built in front of the older nave with side aisles. The contrasting principles – the ground-plan wave of the façade and the straight line of the tower – complement each other in this building, united by the will of one architect.

When Anselmo Lurago added the balcony to the façade of the Černín Palace, he ignored the solid regularity of Caratti's building with its fascinating, repetitive rhythm. The plan of the balcony is derived from a complicated curve, an idea which was foreign and antagonistic to Palladian architecture. On the other hand, he created a rare interplay of consoles, curving surfaces and the cylindrical shape of columns.

The tendency towards unification in Baroque art erased the boundary between sculpture and architecture. Single sculptural motifs permeate architecture, which itself becomes sculpture. The predilection for twisted columns returned, and their dynamics and lively shape competes with the dynamics of statues composed in spiralling movements. The porch frames convey the impression of being modelled from malleable material. As we have seen, even boundary walls, i.e. formations of a purely structural and functional nature, were subjected to this passion for moulding and contrasting of volumes. To this day, some of these still appear as large sculptural compositions in the irregular patchwork of Prague's cityscape. The stone supporting walls and terraces of the Palffy Palace that rise up out of the lush vegetation like monumental crystalline forms, arrest the eye with their stark geometry. Surrounded by fine and cultivated garden architecture, this accumulation of mass achieves the independence of a piece of art, and is one of the results of the struggle of the Baroque architect with his materials. There is no doubt that many of these structures, regardless of the fact that they have often been changed, do not correspond to the accepted notion of Baroque architecture. In their original or altered forms, many of them stand out as impressive pieces of art in the Prague cityscape, thanks to their position in its hilly terrain.

We also find a merging of contrasting principles in the positions Baroque architects take on questions of structure, material and form. The outstanding architects Caratti and Kilián Ignác Dientzenhofer designed two different types of wall, which, though they undoubtedly appear to be closely related to each other are, in subtle ways, diametrically opposed to each other in the way they were built. Caratti designed a sharply cut, diamond-pointed rustication for the base of the Černín Palace. The colossal order gives it rhythm as well as a dimension of depth. The blocks are square, halved in size and oblong. Layers of two blocks alternate with layers of three. The effect, as a whole, is a geometrical play of pyramids, triangles and rhomboids. In full sunlight their shadows also partake and from a certain viewpoint the play of light and shade even dominates the architecture of the entire wall. In the garden villa on Všehrd Street, however, the architect Kilián Ignác Dientzenhofer designed a wall which attests to his knowledge of historical forms. He re-employed an historical motif which we know from Romanesque friezes. The sophistication of this form lies in the fact that a wall structure that was created from the most ordinary and widespread of materials, brick, produces a light effect similar to the one created by the base of the Černín Palace. Notwithstanding this connection, the artistic form of the garden wall of the house on Všehrd Street takes us into a world of completely different structures and rough materials.

In the architecture of the 17th and 18th centuries in Prague, we very often find ordinary lime walls and greatly simplified shapes, a poetry of free, unbound form. The geometrically precise silhouette of dark cannonballs set into the walls of the Capuchin Church on the Hradčany after the bombing of Prague in 1757, the irregular structure of pantiles, the barely formed bud of a cylindrical form of a primitive apse, together with a coarsely plastered boundary wall, form a free group of shapes, surfaces and structures that grew over centuries without a specific unifying idea. These effective sensual compositions presuppose the participation of the beholder. Despite their simplicity, it would be a mistake to attribute them all to a deliberate striving for primitiveness of form.

The side wall of the Church of St Francis of the Order of the Knights of the Cross, on the other hand, is an example of austere, sophisticated and decidedly intellectual emphasis on tectonics, and is constructed by means which belong to the vocabulary of late Mannerism. The wall is given its character by banded rustication, which simulates masonry joints in plaster. The bands are supplemented by flat square, rectangle and rhomboid motifs that, together with the projecting window frames, create a quite peculiar and unclassical combination. A tectonic system of a flat Roman Doric order is incorporated into this graphic play of surfaces and lines as well. The Church of St Francis was designed by Mathey, an architect who had such a masterly command of the order systems that he subtly attempted to act contrary to their rules carefully avoiding a violation of the principles of Mannerist architecture. However, the effect he thus achieved cannot be fully experienced because the wall faces onto a narrow street. Only a photo-montage that vertically mirrors part of the wall, thus extending its articulation, reveals the structure and beauty of its composition.

In this way the dialogue between forms and means of composition found in the works of Prague Baroque architecture enriches and intensifies life in the noisy and vivacious city of today. Here, they continue to live their own lives, full of serenity and discipline, and radiating the dynamics of their materials and forms. To contemporary aesthetic sensibility, which is influenced by the entire art of the 20th century, historical architecture resonates not only as a source of knowledge of the past, but also as an important part of the living artistic universe.

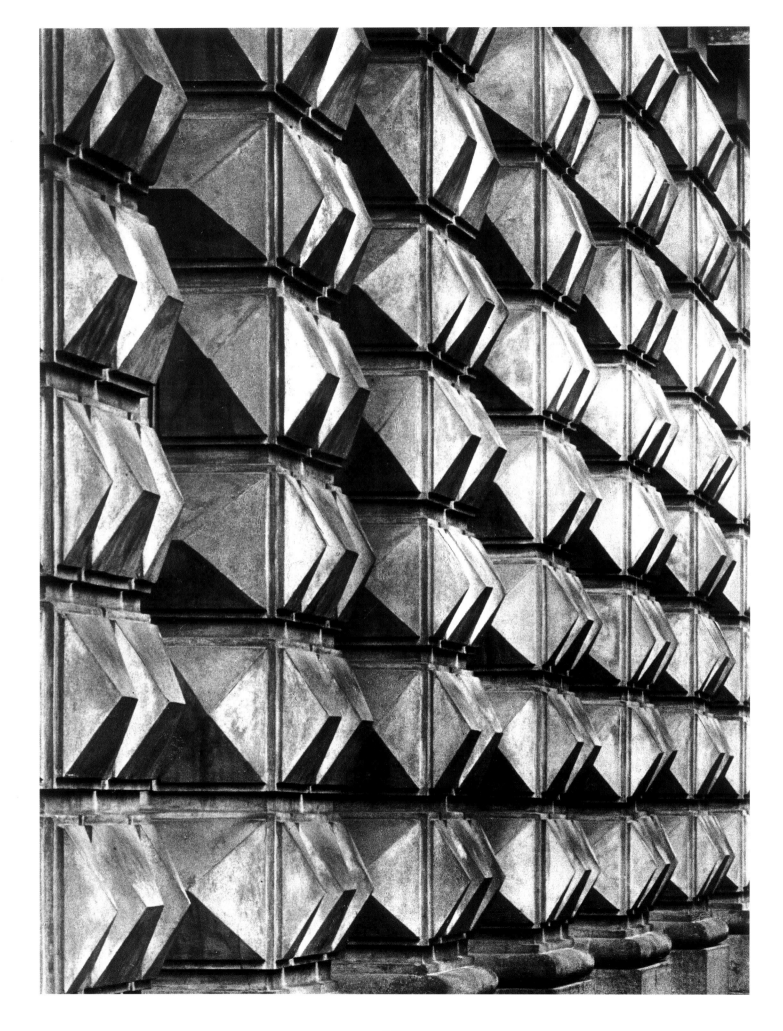

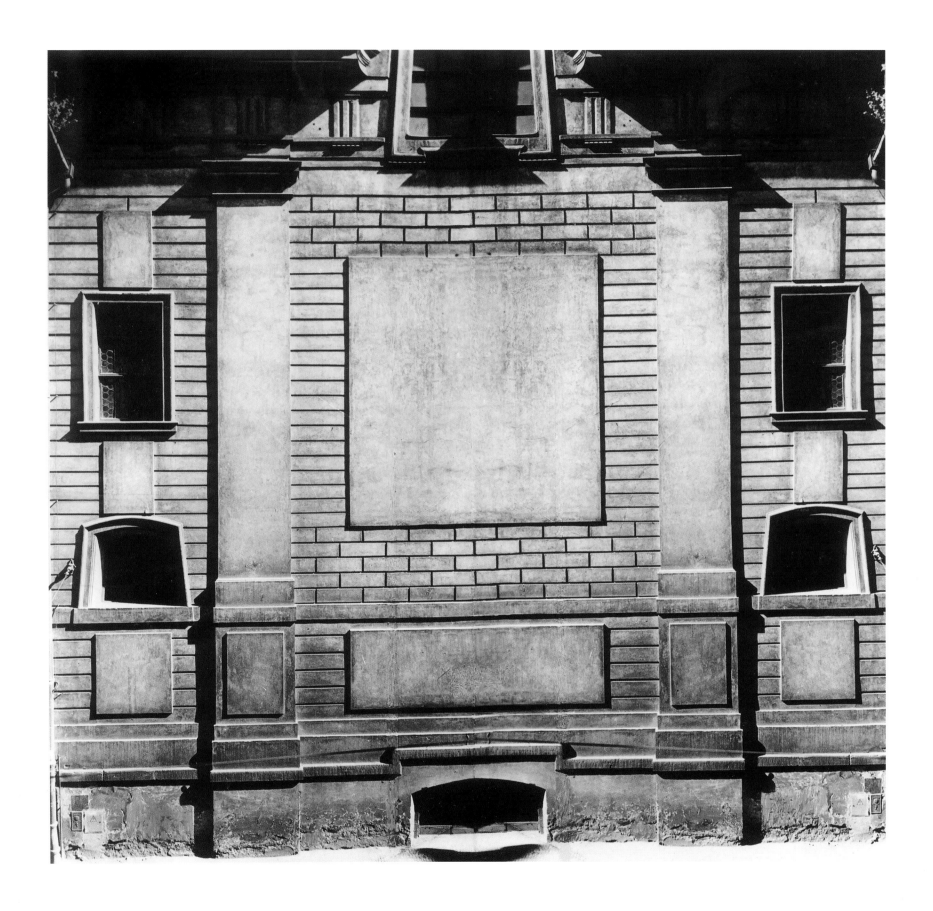

Catalogue

Valdštejn (Wallenstein) Palace
Malá Strana (The Lesser Quarter)

The set of buildings, around five interior courtyards and a large garden, was built for Albrecht of Valdštejn primarily in the period from 1623-30. The houses and land with gardens were gained by the Generalissimo of the Imperial Army through ruthless pressure as early as 1621-22. The main building, facing Valdštejnské (Wallenstein) Square, was designed and built by Andrea Spezza. Following his death in 1628, the project was managed until 1630 by Vincenzo Boccacci[1], and after 1630 by Nicolo Sebregondi. When Valdštejn died on February 25 1634, the palace had not yet been completed due to its extraordinary size.

Valdštejn's chief art adviser for designing the palace sections, and apparently the architect for the design of the garden loggia, was Giovanni Pieroni. The discovery of the plans of the Valdštejn Palace in Bologna and Florence[2] verified Pieroni's role.

The size of the palace reflects the gigantomania in Valdštejn's character, which was equally represented by his social ambitions. Structural details (windows, portals) relate to Mannerism and Late-Renaissance rather than the Baroque style, thus clinging to the past rather than opening a new epoch.

On the other hand, the loggia (finished in 1626) is indicative of an effort for a more complicated expression, evident in the corner grouping of the anta, pilaster and protruding column. The proportions of the Tuscan double column are relatively clear and slender (which is made possible by the wooden vaulting), but the scale is colossal.

Late Renaissance motifs are developed in the interior of the sala terrena, its walls permeated by the rhythm of the ordinary stucco décor compositions, and in the niches (1629-30), with frescoes by Baccio di Bianco. The loggia is followed up with a grotto (built at the same time) and an access corridor with finely profiled ribs and absurd configurations of artificial stalactites that seem to grow from the ribbing.

The garden is enclosed within an architecturally designed wall, which passes in the vicinity of the aviary into a giant wall with artificial stalactite work. This contrasted with the floral décor of the parterre and the noble statues carved by Adriaen de Vries (†1626) and Wurzelbauer's Venus (cast in 1599, mounted on the fountain in 1630; now a copy).

Above left: Valdštejn Palace, present-day appearance
Above Right: Valdštejn Palace, c. 1769 (Engraving by Huber)
Page 167, top: Valdštejn Palace, view of the loggia from the garden
Page 167, bottom: Valdštejn Palace, 2nd quarter of 18th century (Engraving by B.B. Werner)
Below: Valdštejn Palace, plan of the piano nobile with hall and loggia, front wings

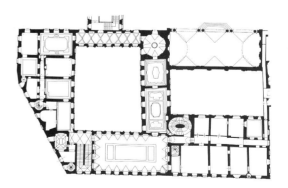

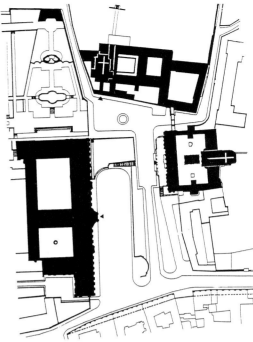

Loreta (The Loreto)
Hradčany (The Castle)

This shrine was built around the Santa Casa, an earlier church that was a copy of a chapel in the Italian town of Loreto. The construction of the Santa Casa was funded by Benigna Catherina of Lobkovic. The foundation stone was laid on June 3, 1626. The architect Giovanni Battista Orsi brought the structure into a usable state a year later, though the chapel was not consecrated until 1631. The rich stucco decoration that can still be seen on the western façade was carried out by Jacopo Agosto in 1664, and was a replacement of earlier chiaroscuro paintings. The stuccowork was then entrusted to Giovanni Battista Colombo, and after him to Giovanni Bartolomeo Cometa, who completed it. In 1795 F. Kunz decorated the interior with imitations of fragments of older paintings.

Surrounding the Santa Casa chapel is a cloister (1634, Giovanni Battista Orsi) with two bell-towers (from 1644 Andrea Allio, and 1648 Silvestro Carlone). The chapels in the corners were added gradually: 1685-86 the Chapel of Our Lady of Sorrows, 1687 the Chapel of St Anne (Jan Jiří Mayer), 1691 the Chapel of St Joseph

and the Holy Rood, 1710-12 the Chapel of St Anthony of Padua. Kryštof Dientzenhofer also built the Chapel of St Francis of Seraphin in 1717, and in 1718 adapted the Chapel of the Nativity of Christ – the oratory. The Chapel of St Anthony of Padua was enlarged by Dientzenhofer in 1722-23 by an extension into the courtyard, and remodelled once again by the builder Jan Jiří Aichbauer in 1734-37. The organ was built in 1734-38 by Josef Helwig. Another storey was added to the cloister by Kilián Ignác Dientzenhofer in 1746-47. The Loreto front wing facing Loretánské (Loreto Square was begun by Kryštof Dientzenhofer under a contract dated February 21 1721. Stonecarving work was executed by J.V. Mannes[3]. The façade of the front wing was completed in 1723 by Kilián Ignác Dientzenhofer. The adjoining terrace was adapted in 1725-26 by Kilián Ignác Dientzenhofer. The putti on the balustrade were carved by Ondřej Filip Quittainer in 1725-26 (now replaced with copies). Two stucco reliefs were added to the façade in the same period. They are the work of Jan Bedřich Kohl-Severa.

Above left: Loreta, 2nd quarter of 18th century (Engraving by B.B. Werner)
Above: Loretánské (Loreto) Square with the Černin Palace (left), Capuchin Monastery (centre) and Lorata (right)
Page 169: Loreta, façade, present-day appearance (top); Church of the Nativity of Christ (middle); Santa Casa (bottom)
Pages 170–171: Loretánské (Loreto) Square with the Černín Palace, Capuchin Monastery (centre), and Lorata (Drawing by Leopold Peuker)

The Matthias Portal at Prague Castle
Hradčany (The Castle)

The Theresian reconstruction of the Prague Castle, based on the plans of the architect Nicolo Pacassi (after 1762), with the participation of architects Anselmo Lurago and Antonín Kunz (from 1766), included the addition of the Matthias Portal, named after Emperor Matthias, the successor of Rudolf II, into the entrance wing of the Castle. According to Ehemant and Schaller, and judging from an analysis of the style, the design of this truly monumental gateway can be attributed to the architect Vincenzo Scamozzi[4], who stayed in Prague from August 1599 until May 1600.

In 1613 the construction was entrusted to architect Giovanni Maria Filippi. The groundwork for the foundations was, however, laid out as early as 1607[5]. The possibility that Filippi visited architect Scamozzi during a trip to Italy and consulted with him about the project, is regarded as improbable[6]. Scamozzi himself never mentioned the Matthias Portal. No evidence of Scamozzi's involvement has been found in the Castle archives so far[7].

An outstanding feature of the gateway composition is its being based on precisely assembled combinations of order architecture with the technique of wall design, accentuated by means of rustication. It corresponds with the means of expression used by the architects Sanmicheli and Scamozzi in the Venice region, and described by Serlio in his fourth book.

The solemn Roman Doric order runs through two storeys, and is covered with conspicuously profiled and structured rustication which at some points pass into the arch. The massive triple voussoirs, the largest one in the middle pointing at the axis of the openings, underline the fortress-like impression produced by the structure. The upper extension of the gable, with two side pylons, stretches over two storeys of Paccasi's wing. The theory of superposition in order architecture recommends the use of a lighter order in the upper storey – the Ionic order was chosen in this case. In between the two flat pilasters, the architect offered space which was used for the inscription D.MATTHIAS.F.L.ROM.IMP.S.AUG.HUNG.BOH.REX2CFF.A NO.MDCXIV.

The design of the gable above the main cornice differs markedly from that of the ground level, presumably due to the intervention of another architect.

Above: Matthias Portal, first courtyard of Prague Castle 1791-1792 (Engraving by Filip und Fr. Heger)
Page 171, top: Matthias Portal, detail
Page 171, bottom: Mathias Portal, entry area

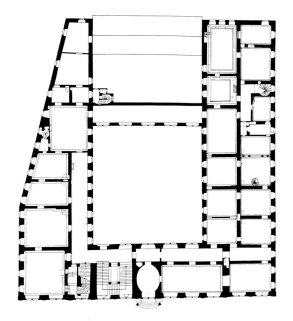

Nostic Palace
Malá Strana (The Lesser Quarter)

The foundation stone was laid in 1660. The project was ordered by Jan Hartvík, Count of Nostic, who had two variations of the plans prepared[8]. In 1662, he obtained permission to use public land[9] and land under the jurisdiction of the Maltese Order.

The layout of the palace was redesigned in 1736, as was the northern façade. The portal was added some time around 1760. The windows of the second storey were later altered to conform with Classicist taste. The masks in the high-order capitals, which were the reason for originally attributing the palace to the architect Francesco Caratti, are actually the work of an unknown architect, since they were executed after 1662.

The analogy of the colossal order design of the Nostic Palace with that of the Černín Palace at Hradčany is, however, disputable in many respects. The differences include the placement of flat pilasters on the base at ground floor level, the entire architrave, the frieze and the cornice, the shape of the doubled windows, and the loosened rhythmic division.

The Nostic Palace thus shows much greater affinity with the solution chosen by Carlo Lurago for the Clementinum[10]. Besides, it was not always the case that the architect also designed the ornamental part of the stucco decoration. However, the report of Vilímková[11] claims that Caratti is named as the architect of the Nostic Palace in the archives of Český Krumlov. This statement cannot be verified at present, but is significant in determining the architect of the palace. Architectural analysis, nonetheless, speaks in favours Carlo Lurago as the author.

Left, from top to bottom: Nostic Palace, 1st-floor plan; façade; detail of a capital

Above right: Nostic Palace, 2nd quarter of the 18th century (Engraving by B.B. Werner)

Michna Palace
Malá Strana (The Lesser Quarter)

Originally a Renaissance structure, Pavel Michna of Vacínov had it rebuilt before the middle of the 17th century and enlarged by the addition of a garden wing, of which only a shell has remained. The generous, late Renaissance design of the main front was to be developed along the entire façade, but this idea was implemented only in part. The original intention of the architect is evident from the plan found in the Dientzenhofer sketchbook[12]. The unusual, conspicuously protuberant middle façade is unsteadily counterbalanced by three-aisled passages running through both parallel wings, across the inside courtyards (the wings actually are divergent). The façade on the garden side reflects a conflict of several architectural ideas, resulting in a highly unusual series of openings, uncompleted linkages and opposing forces. At the same time, however, a surface area was created which is interesting for its uncommon, haphazard and loose composition, and is impressive as a whole.

The stylistic starting point for the structure is Roman, the design of the main front façade and the adjacent axis corresponds with the composition of the façade by Alessandro Algardi's Villa Doria-Pamphili, built at about the same time. It was once attributed to Francesco Caratti but was disproved by the finding of a letter written by Caratti himself[13], saying that he had not entered the services of the Michna family until the year of 1657. The construction took place in 1644-45, when the Michnas employed the stonemason, Zacharias Bussi, and plasterer, Domenico Galli. In 1767, the palace was purchased by the State and converted into a military arsenal. In 1922, the devastated building was acquired by the Czech Sokol Association (a sporting organization) and transformed into a sports centre. Krásny (with the scientific assistance of Professor V. Birnbaum) designed its reconstruction in the style of Riegl's analytic Viennese school.

Above, from left to right: Michna Palace; the building in about. 1769 (Engraving by Huber); plan of the piano nobile, 1st floor.

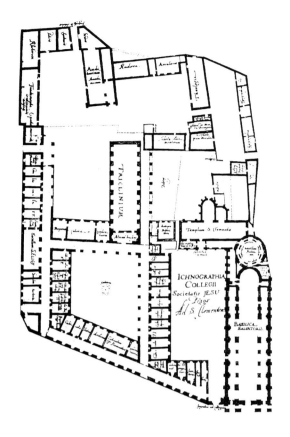

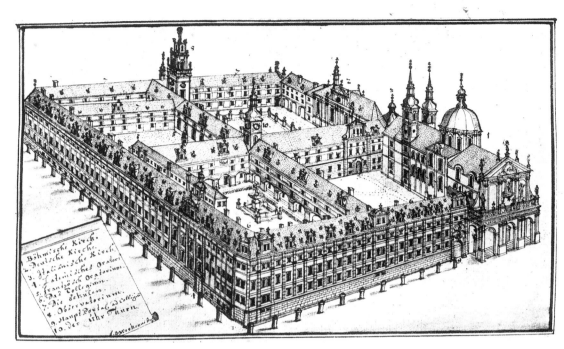

The Church of The Holy Savior and the Western Wing of the Clementinum
Staré Město (The Old Town)

The complex of the Clementinum (former Jesuit College, university, and finally the National and Technical Libraries) occupies the whole block between Křižovnická Street, Karlova Street, Mariánské Square and Platnéřská Street. The set of buildings is complemented by two churches (The Holy Savior's and St Clement's) and three chapels. A Dominican monastery, 'situated at the foot of the bridge', existed here from the 13th century. In 1554, it was chosen by Peter Canisius as the seat of the Jesuit Order in The Old Town of Prague. The Church of The Holy Savior itself was reconstructed by the Jesuits between 1578 and 1582. The reconstruction involved adaptations of a part of the former Dominican church, the insertion of perhaps two wooden tribunes and two towers. The nave, respecting the original plan of a nave and two side aisles, was erected in 1600 on older foundations. The unusually long space was enriched with a dome surmounting two thirds of the crossing; its construction was however postponed until the early Baroque period. The project was managed in 1600-1601 by Marek Fontana, with Boniface Wohlmuth possibly collaborating on the late Renaissance concept. The structure displays prominent elements testifying to the power of the Gothic tradition in the Czech Lands (Bohemia, Moravia, and Silesia), as well as attractive manifestations of neo-Renaissance formal systems, known from model books (i.e. the Renaissance marble entry portal, 1601).

The original façade, known from early prints, is now concealed behind the new composition of the loggia. As an immediate follow-up (in 1590-1600), the remarkable Vlašská (Italian) Chapel was built at the end of the Church of The Holy Savior, with a slight shift of the axis. The chapel has an oval plan and two-storey interior galleries. Krčálová (1989) ascribes the authorship of this edifice to the papal architect Ottavio Mascherini[14]. After 1640 the second, early Baroque, phase of the remodelling of the Holy Savior's Church started. The crossing was surmounted with the monastery vault (1649), built on the timber-framed structure of a polygonal tambour; but after 1740, the vault had to be taken down because of a defective structure.

The foundation stone for the new part of St Clement's College was laid in 1653. Two contracts were signed (in 1654 and 1655) with the architect and owner of a prosperous building company, Carlo Lurago, who pledged to finish the construction of the western wing up to the roof by the end of 1655. A contract concluded in 1656, provided for the pilasters to be framd and ornamented with blocks ('bugne')'. This led Vilímková[15] to assume that the conspicuous banding (rustication) of the pilasters was not a part of the original design but a later intervention. Under the next contract of 1660, Carlo Lurago built the wing from the corner at Platnéřská Street to the Church of St Eligius inclusive. Further contracts were signed in 1665, and 1669, (also involving Francesco Lurago). They were considerably detailed, defining even the thickness of the walls (about 2 m). A wooden model of the structure was even

made. The architect cannot be determined for certain, either by style analyses or by the fact that the contract stipulated that Carlo Lurago would build according to plans supplied to him. In 1668, Carlo Lurago left for Passau. The subsequent contract of 1679 was concluded with architect G. Dom. Orsi. The western façade, whose value in terms of proportion was reduced later on when the base portion was covered over, is now underground. Yet it still is probably the most developed rhythmic composition to be seen in Prague. The vertical motifs of the colossal order rusticated pilasters (with an interesting slant of the plan at the points from which oblique corridors run in the interior) alternate with the band of windows. Horizontal binding links and cordoned cornices penetrate the vertical rhythm, so that all elements are 'intertwined' in a complicated manner. The wide variety of form is further enhanced by the massive cornices above the windows, by sculptural capitals (plasterer Giovanni Bartolomeo Cometa) and the weight of the cornice and dormer windows. This precise composition became the target of criticism on the part of the Jesuit Order leadership right

after its completion, and therefore was not repeated elsewhere on the façades, which were considerably simpler.

The photographs in this book were inspired by the western façade of the Clementinum and by the loggia which was added in 1653-59 to the Holy Saviour's Church front of an earlier date.

The three-arched loggia is based on the motif of a triumphal gateway. Yet it differs from the monumental façade of the neighbouring Clementinum in terms of scale, structure, decorative elements, and in the use of progressive technical ideas – i.e. the so-called Bohemian vault. Since a contribution was made for the cost of the church construction by Count Michna of Vacínov, the hypothesis appeared that the inventive efforts of architect Fr. Caratti may have been engaged, too. But Caratti had not entered the service of Count Michna until 1657[16], and therefore could have neither designed nor built the loggia. Despite the conceptual differences with the adjacent Clementinum, the authorship of the loggia can, therefore, be justifiably ascribed to Carlo Lurago[17]. Preiss regards the probable

model as Lodovico Cigoli's proposed design for the façade of S. Maria del Fiore in Florence[18].

The entire Clementinum complex underwent a series of later restylings, which alone merit a separate study. (The new construction stage after 1709, the laying of the foundation stone for the Church of St Clement in 1712, the High Baroque reconstruction of the section facing towards Mariánské Square in 1719, the construction of the astronomy tower in 1722, the Mirror Chapel in 1722-23 etc.) Between 1924 and 1962, the Clementinum was reconstructed by Ladislav Machoň to serve as libraries and university reading rooms, which it still does today.

Above left: Church of Holy Savior, façade
Above: Clementinum, façade
Page 176, left: Clementinum, plan, original design, 1696 (Ichnographia Collegii Sociatatis Jesu Praga ad S. Clementem)
Page 176, right: Clementinum, 2nd quarter of the 18th century (Drawing by B.B. Werner)

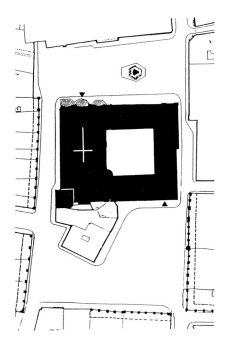

The Jesuits' Monastic House
Malá Strana (The Lesser Quarter)

In the place of two churches, a presbytery (the parish priest's residence), the former townhall, a school, Ševcovská Street and several town houses, a structure was erected in the middle of Lesser Quarter Square, the history of which represents one of the most interesting topics in the study of town development in the 17th century[19]. In 1623, the idea of settling the Jesuits in the immediate neighbourhood of the St Nicholas Church emerged. The church, presbytery, school and houses attached to the church were handed over to the Jesuit Order in 1625.

Preliminary discussions about the new construction project did not start until 1653, after the church and the houses had been adapted and funds had been raised. A surviving draft of the agreement made at that time between the Jesuits and The Lesser Quarter municipality, provides for the replacement of the Gothic tower by a new one, and proposes two design variations that rely on changing the lay of the street, to the disadvantage of municipal land. Under an agreement of 1654, the street was moved as much as nine metres westwards, and the location of the new tower was defined – at the place where it actually stands today. But building did not start for quite some time – despite major

financial subsidies, bequeathed by Václav Libštejn of Kolovraty and others. Intensive negotiations continued until 1673.

The principle of austerity of architectural expression was already asserted in the preparatory phases. In 1667, the Prague Jesuits' superiors recommended that the structure be kept simple, and in 1673 the General of the Order P. Oliva demanded in a letter to provost P.V. Hermann that the overly ornate Clementinum College should not be used as the model for the new project. The municipality managed to resist the Jesuits' demands until March 1673, when a compromise was finally reached. Plans no doubt existed for the purpose of the negotiations, and were used several times to stake out the site. The names of Dominico (Domenico Orsi de Orsini) and Jan Blažej Santini, who took the measurements of the plot of land, are mentioned. Apart from the existing variations of the plan, a concept proposal was presented soon after the contract signing in March 1673, by Francesco Caratti, supported by Count Černín. The foundation stone of the church was laid on September 6, 1673. Demolition work followed, and by 1674 the front wall of the church had been built up to ground level. The construction was supervised by a P. Bos, himself a member of the Jesuit Order. Because no remnants of the earlier structures had been preserved, and because the construction pit for the Monastic House had to be excavated, on the eastern side, down

to the level of the second basement, it is clear that (except for the foundation wall and excavation of the pit) the project had not progressed far by 1676, due to the large scale of these works. On March 17, 1676, a new contract was signed with G.D. Orsi de Orsini, leaving him to continue with the construction according to his plan. After Orsi's death in 1679, the project was contracted to Francesco Lurago. When comparing the plans from the Bibliothèque Nationale, the plan in Heintsch's portrait of Count Libštejn of Kolovraty, and a layout sketch of 1673 with the reality of the preserved Romanesque and Renaissance St Václav (Wenceslas) Church, and considering the fact that the decision to pull down the church was not made until 1683, it can be assumed that the author of the Parisian plans was F. Lurago, while it is clearly Orsi's concept that is represented in the portrait painted by Heintsch. Another argument in favour of this hypothesis is the change in the northern, western and eastern façades. The eastern wing was completed in 1680, the northern and western ones in 1690.

Above left: The Jesuits' Monastic House, plan
Above right: The Jesuits' Monastic House, c. 1769 (Engraving from Huber's Orthography)
Page 179: The Jesuits' Monastic House

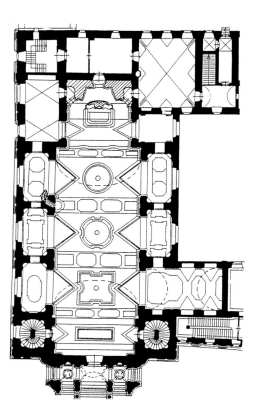

The Church of St Ignatius
Nové Město (The New Town)

The history of the construction of this major 17th-century Jesuit church in Prague has several phases. As early as 1622, Emperor Ferdinand II donated the Corpus Christi Church on Dobytčí trh (Cattle Marketplace, present-day Karlovo – Charles – Square) to the Clementinum College, which had been administered since 1403 by Prague University. The church stood on the square directly opposite the present day St Ignatius Church. The Jesuits would have preferred the former Koňsky trh (Horse Marketplace, today Václavské (Wenceslas) Square as the location, as they regarded it as more central. The authorities, however, refused to permit such a change. In much the same way as in the case of the Jesuits' residences in the Old Town and Lesser Quarters, the design of the New Town College (its first phase erected between 1658 and 1667 in the

southern part of an enormous construction site that occupied the entire half of the southeastern side of the present day Karlovo Square included a church, added at the corner of the square and Žitná Street.

Accounting documents relating to the church construction and dating back to 1665 still exist. The first report about walls erected 'to a man's height', is given by P.J. Miller in his history of the Jesuit Order until 1665[20]. The project leader was Carlo Lurago, Dominico Luragoni (Lurago) was the foreman, the stonemasons were Martin Cech and Václav Knaurek, and the name of the carpenter was Kilián Gabriel.

In 1665, Martino Rano (Rainer) was paid 6 guilders for the drawing of the new church. The structure was, however, executed by the Jesuit builder Carlo Lurago. A considerable variety of alternative plans have been preserved[21], as well as annual reports (Annuae), and the project accounting documents.

The design was carried out in several stages: the 1st stage from 1665 to 1678 – the consecration; 1683-5 –

the All Souls' Chapel, or Chapel of the Deceased; 1686 – the choir (possibly already with the participation of Pavel Ignác Bayer). Carlo Lurago was replaced as the project leader in 1671, by Martino Rano. In 1671, the 'extremely high walls' were surmounted with a vault, the majority of the sculptural elements were finished, the roof was covered with tiles, and the small tower was covered with tin and furnished with a gilded dome. The façade of the front was decorated up to half its height. The top was crowned with the dignified stone statue of St Father Ignatius, surrounded by a gold-plated nimbus combined with four shining gilded spheres. According to the annual report of 1672, the sculptural decoration including the mounting of the obelisks was finished in that year.

In 1676, with building work already under the leadership of Martino Rano, the vault was decorated with a 'sculpture work of rare elegance'. On July 31, 1678, the church was consecrated by the Prague Archbishop of that time, Jan Bedřich of Valdštejn.

The tower was built in 1687 by Pavel Ignác Bayer, who also added the front portico in 1697-99. The sacristy and the oratory were surmounted with a vault in 1715. Attributing the concept to an architect is difficult, due to an abundance of conflicting reports. Documents found in the cupola testify in favour of the 'architects' Martino Rano and Pavel Ign. Bayer, while preserved plans obviously come from several design studios. Except for one bearing the signature of Pavel Ignác Bayer, the plans are unsigned.

Apart from the undisputed involvement of Pavel Ignác Bayer (under the influence of Pozzo) as the designer of the portico, further possible authors stated in literature are Giovanni Dom. Orsi and Carlo Lurago, of whom the latter probably not only executed but also designed the project.

The stuccowork of marvellous form and richness was made by Tomasso Soldati[22].

The church façade was restored in 1895. The outside plaster, including the stucco ornamentation, was removed and reworked. The main cornice, including that of the portico, was also remade. The sculptures were replaced with copies, and new ones were added on the portico. The stucco decoration was cleaned and enriched. However, this was a poor restoration (see the report by Prof. Guth, Matějček), and work had to be carried out again between 1916 and 1939, and between 1946 and 1990.

The dèsign of the unusually extensive single nave with side chapels and a tribune, is derived from the Il Gesù Church in Rome, though it differs considerably in its layout (which is not centrally planned), the lighting conditions, the articulation of the side wall (inserted tribunes, discontinued entablature), and the combination of stucco decoration with columns

Page 180, from left to right: The Church of St Ignatius, exterior, plan, interior
Above left: Cattle Marketplace c. 1785 (Engraving by J. Balzer, drawing by J.A. Scotti de Cassano)
Above: Detail from a panorama of Prague, 1680-1685, the New Town College with the church and the Chapel of Corpus Christi (Engraving by Folpertus van Ouden-Allen)

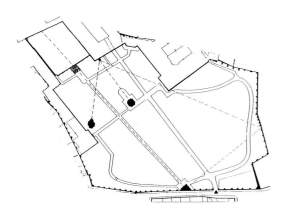

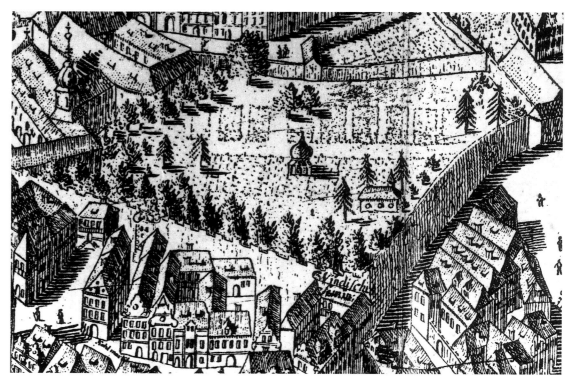

The Chapel of St Elijah
Vojanovy Park
Malá Strana (The Lesser Quarter)

In 1655, Emperor Ferdinand II purchased the whole palace and its adjacent property from the Counts of Valdštejn, intending to use it for a new Carmelite convent. The property was defined in the contract as a park, flower and vegetable gardens, and orchards. In addition to the property purchased from the Valdštejns, the Emperor also used the garden that had originally belonged to the Flavín family, and which had been confiscated as punishment for the owners' involvement in the Czech Estates uprising. The extensive area of land was situated on The Lesser Quarter bank of the Vltava River; the site was called 'Na písku' ('On The Sands'). The traditional garden with an orchard, mentioned as early as 1336, was probably already part of the property adjoining the bishop's seat near the bridge at the end of the 13th century. Excavations on the banks revealed

Romanesque and early Gothic foundations of a fortress that had existed near the ramparts and entry to the Judith Bridge, the predecessor of Charles Bridge. The bishop's seat bordered on the Gothic wall of The Lesser Quarter[23]. In 1668-76 the garden was enclosed with a high wall. Though for a long time it was probably purely a utility garden, its design clearly reveals a Baroque influence. This can be seen in the terraces (built around 1680); the trident of the garden axes oriented on the oriel of the convent building, its focus being the Chapel of St Theresa (1743-45); the Chapel of St Elijah, which is designed as a grotto (from the third quarter of the 17th century); and a chapel (that no longer exists) over the grave of St Electa. This axial ideology is combined with prominent architectural axes: an axis connecting the stairway with the trilateral Chapel of St John of Nepomuk (the third quarter of the 17th century), and another perpendicular axis running from the side of this chapel, at present indistinct in the layout of the garden.

The interior of the Chapel of St Elijah rises above a plan in the form of a cross, its arms slanting at an unusual angle, and surmounted with barrel vaulting, which is obscured by grotto motifs such as small stones, slivers of glass and shells (with snakes crawling out of the holes). The vault is decorated with frescoes. A beautiful statue of the prophet Elijah by Jan Antonín Geiger once stood in the centre. The entry is furnished with a relief of the Habsburg Eagle, the Chain of the Golden Fleece and the symbol of the Carmelites. The masonry of the grotto is an amorphous formation, with stalactites and a lava-like surface[24].

Above left: Vojanovy Park, layout
Above right: Vojanovy Park, c. 1769 (Engraving from Huber's Orthography)

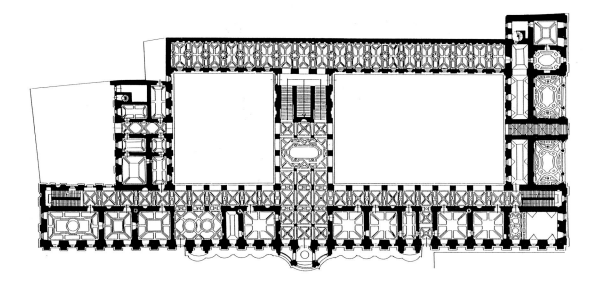

Top: Černín Palace, ground floor plan

Above: Černín Palace, 2nd quarter of the 18th century

(Engraving by B.B. Werner)

Above right: Černín Palace, view

Černín (Czernin) Palace
Hradčany (The Castle)

Following the acquisition of the houses belonging to the Lobkovic family in 1666, the final decision was made by Humprecht Jan Černín to build the monumental palace that we know today. Gianlorenzo Bernini probably drew up the plans for this structure in 1666. M. Ceresolo was followed by Francesco Caratti as the architect who actually implemented the extraordinary concept of the palace, in keeping with his client's vision.

The architect Francesco Caratti, who was employed by the Lobkovic family until 1656[25], and later – until his death – by the Michnas for the Church of St Mary

Magdalene in The Lesser Quarter, presented the first (unpreserved) variation of the plans at the beginning of 1668. Toward the end of that year, the project was contracted to Giovanni da Capauli and Abraham Leuthner. Caratti offered his services to Humprecht Jan Černín at the end of 1667, and was employed in 1669[26]. After the approval of the (partially preserved) plans drawn by Caratti in 1668 and 1669, the project progressed at such a pace that by 1673 the basic structure was ready. When architect Francesco Caratti died in 1677, the façades were already decorated with stucco-work by Giovanni Maderna, Giovanni Bartolomeo Cometa, Francesco Perri and Antonio Travelli[27]. The architect Giovanni Battista Maderna, and after him, until 1696, Domenico Egidio Rossi, participated in the final stage of the construction.

The interior of the palace was adapted by František Maxmilián Kaňka between 1718 and 1722. After being pillaged by the French, the palace was repaired by Anselmo Lurago.

The curvilinear balcony, built in 1747-50 according to the design of A. Lurago and the model of Ignaz Platzer, contrasts with the austere Palladian forms of the front façade – differing in style, yet with a definite artistic effect.

The redesign of the floors of the main wing by Achille Wolf (in 1855-56) was to the detriment of the façade and the interiors. The palace restoration project of 1928-34, conducted by Pavel Janák, while no doubt saving the palace from ruin was slave to the conservationist theory of that time, adding new forms of the window aedicules, parapets and ornament to the front. Only the base, the colossal order with the cornice, the basic positioning of the windows in the upper storeys, and a part of the morphology remained preserved from Caratti's project[28].

Above left: Černín Palace, design of the main hall decoration, Domenico Egidio Rossi, 1696

Page 185, top left: Černín Palace, ceiling, design

Page 185, top right: Černín Palace, vestibule

Page 185, bottom: Černín Palace, garden (Photo: Arch. Otakar Fierlinger)

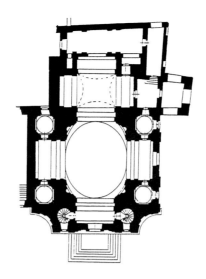

The Church of St Francis of the Order of the Knights of the Cross
Staré Město (The Old Town)

The church ranks among the supreme works of architecture in Prague in terms of its location, the composition of its exterior, the design of the interior, as well as the sculptural and painted decorations, the furnishings and the materials used. It was built according to the plans of the French architect Jean-Baptiste Mathey in 1679-88.

The architectural value of the Church of St Francis exceeds that of Jean-Baptiste Mathey's other large-scale compositions, and ranks above the contemporary creations both in terms of a new approach to the plan (two ovals with mutually perpendicular main axes, chamfering on the outside in the diagonal, etc.), and because of a masterful treatment of the forms of late Mannerism, which made it possible to abandon established schemes, loosen the tectonic bonds of architectural orders, and treat details of the whole with the outstanding skill and finesse of a connoisseur of Roman academic architecture of the mid-17th century.

Plans from the archives of the Order of the Knights of the Cross, published by Sádlo[29], testify to the fact that the resultant composition was not the outcome of a gradual refinement of a single idea. Five of the published plans are not directly connected with each other (except for plans No. 4 and 5). On the contrary, there were considerable fluctuations in quality, and the final version was chosen justifiably.

Difficulties posed by the building site were similar to those of the adjacent convent (Carlo Lurago from 1661). This used to be the location of the Church of the Holy Ghost, which was pulled down only in part. Its sub-

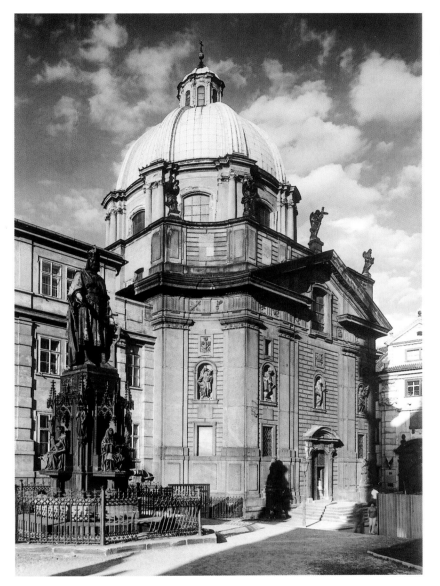

structures, adapted by Jean-Baptiste Mathey and decorated with stalactite motifs, were preserved in the basement. The structure, nonetheless, has survived in good condition until the present day, which testifies to the expertise of the builder (Gaudenzio Casanova?[30]) and the architect[31].

The supreme artistic feat is, of course, the way the church fits into the townscape, the panorama of the city, and the manner in which it blends with the composition of the Knights of the Cross Square. In a sophisticated manner, the mass of the church, its scale and rhythm, and the architectural elements of the façades

fulfil this task.

Jean-Baptiste Mathey added, after 1679, a structure to the older architectural monuments at the entrance to the Charles Bridge (i.e. Peter Parler's Bridge Tower on the Old Town side – after 1357, and Lurago's vestibule of the Church of The Holy Savior – after 1653), which is self-contained, but at the same time harmonious with its surroundings in such a remarkable way, that the Knights of the Cross Square is one of the most beautiful in Prague.

Above left: The Church of St Francis of the Order of the Knights of the Cross, façade onto the Knights of the Cross Square
Above: Interior
Page 186, top: The Church of St Francis of the Order of the Knights of the Cross, plan
Page 186, left: Panorama
Page 186, right: Engraving from 2nd quarter of the 18th century (by B.B. Werner)

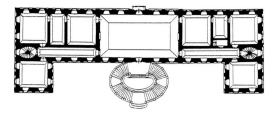

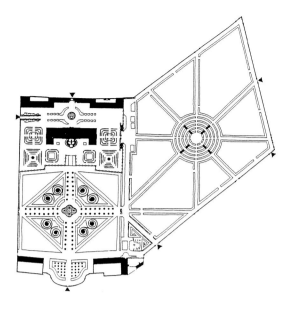

The Troja Summer Palace
Prague 7

The Troja Summer Palace is a highpoint of nature cultivated in a semi-urban setting. The entire site is walled in and surrounded by a large terraced garden and an orchard. An orangery, together with the farm buildings, form an inseparable part of the whole complex. The composition of the garden makes use of its axes, symmetrical sets, vistas and decorative 'prospects', employing illusive architectural means to extend the axes and vistas into an idealized natural setting. The appearance of the summer palace is reminiscent of the villa suburbana, the Italian suburban palace, which was a place of seasonal sojourn for the owners and their guests. The vicinity of the Stromovka royal game preserve, and the splendid interiors of the palace, made it a suitable place for hosting partners in diplomatic negotiations. However, the rooms were never put to their intended use, due to the economic decline of the family that built the palace. The property, with the farm of Zadní Ovenec (the name 'Troja' was not used until the early 18th century) was owned by Count Václav Vojtěch of Šternberk (Sternberg), an educated

and ambitious aristocrat with a cultured outlook, which he gained as a young man during his travels to major European centres[32].

The construction was started by the Prague builder Dominico Orsi de Orsini (†1679), and for the first eight years was supervised by the heir of the firm of Silvestro Carloni. The authorship of the project is claimed by Baptiste Mathey, in a document of June 23 1686, signed by Jean-Baptiste Mathey himself. Mathey, a painter and architect who was born in Burgundy and trained in Rome, was brought to Prague by the Archbishop of Prague, Jan Bedřich of Valdštejn, and charged with designing the Archbishop's Palace, the Church of St Francis on the Knights of the Cross Square, and other structures. Mathey, however, was not a member of the Masons' and Bricklayers' Guild, and under the regulations of that time was not allowed to implement his projects. This was the reason why, in the case of the Troja Summer Palace project, he entered into an unsuccessful conflict with the Guild, and in particular fought with the builder charged with the project, S. Carloni, who even denied Mathey the authorship of the project[33]. But because Mathey was indisputedly the architect working for both the Archbishop and Count Šternberk, and considering the fact that probes made

during recent restoration works did not reveal any changes in the project, he can be regarded as the author of the whole concept, as well as the architect of the project details[34]. The complex has not been preserved in its entirety. The western part, an orchard, was donated to the Prague Zoo.

The governing axis of the entire composition runs through the middle of the palace. It is oriented on Prague Castle, the ideological and architectural dominant in Prague. Turning the composition against the terrain increased cost of the project considerably. The earth that had to be removed was used for the terrace. A visitor entering the palace proceeded along the axis of the official entrance from the south (from the Vltava River). The architectural and artistic resources improve as one proceeds towards the palace. The visitor passes by the propylaeum of the orangeries, the reconstructed fountain in the lower parterre, with vistas opening up diagonally as well as the transversely. The original ornamental parterre (see the engraving based on Werner's drawing from approximately 1740) has been only partially reconstructed, and just a trace of it can be seen today. By way of a bank, the visitor comes to the upper terrace, and after ascending the stairway, reaches the dominant point of the composi-

tion, the main hall. Looking back, one sees (from above) the entire geometrical design of the garden, and a view of the ideological counterpoint of the composition, the panorama of Prague Castle, from a distance of about 3 km.

Fulfilling the challenging task of depicting the Fall of the Giants into the Abyss of the Tartarus was entrusted to two adherents of Berninism, Johann Georg Heermann, and his nephew Paul, artists from Dresden. They created a massive gigantomachia (1685-1703). The balustrade was later mounted with busts from the Brokoff workshop. The artistic and ideological focus of the composition is the Imperial Hall. The architect fully subjugated the space, covering two storeys, to painted decoration. No architectural or sculptural element of the stuccowork stood in the way of an unrestrained pursuit of this intent. The brothers Abraham and Isaac Godyns, invited by Count Šternberk in 1690 to execute the challenging task of decorating the walls and the ceiling of the main hall, paid tribute to the

Habsburg family and the triumphant Catholic Church with brilliant frescoes. The victory of Emperor Leopold over the Turks is presented in the classical style. The frescoes on the ceiling are dated 1693. The distich testifies to the completion of the wall paintings on October 26, 1697, soon after the Battle of Zenta. The victory in this battle was reinforced by the triumphant Battle of Vienna (1683). The hero, the Polish King Jan Sobiesky, is shown in the ceiling fresco. A written ideological programme for the paintings has been found[35]. The Godyns were also responsible for the frescoes of the magnificent stables (the western part of the farm buildings), with their marble details (cf the Baroque cult of thoroughbred horses.)

The less talented painter Francesco Marchetti and his son Giovanni also participated in the decoration of the palace. The unique decoration of the terraces with terrazzo vases (now approximate copies of the originals, which are kept in the depository of the UMPRUM museum) were probably made by the modeller Bombelli.

The palace was renovated in 1977-90. Today it is used as a municipal gallery.

Above: Troja Summer Palace, 2nd quarter of the 18th century (Engraving by B.B. Werner)
Page 188, top left: Ground floor plan
Page 188, left: The building after the reconstruction
Page 188, centre: The Imperial Room
Page 188, right: Layout of the garden

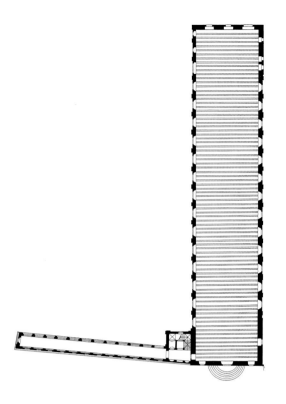

The Prague Castle Riding School
Hradčany (The Castle)

The Czech Chamber, represented by its President Count Šlik, decided in 1694 to build an Imperial Riding School at Prague Castle. The drawing of the plans was entrusted, according to an extant document[36], to architect Jean-Baptiste Mathey, who was widely respected for his designing skills as well as his personal qualities. Mathey promptly drew the plans; the construction was started and the basic structure finished in 1694. The Prague Castle Building Authority selected an old tournament ground near the pheasantry beyond Jelení příkop (Deer Trench, a game preserve) as the site for the riding school project.

The finishing work took place in 1695. The interior originally had a flat ceiling decorated with stuccowork. Mathey supplied the plasterer J.P. Palliardi with detailed drawings of the ornament (warfare weaponry, busts of Turks, a jumping horse – motifs celebrating the victory of the imperial army over the Turks).

After Mathey's departure from the Czech Lands and subsequent death at the turn of 1695/6, the project and the finishing work was managed by Giacomo Antonio Canevalle, who clearly respected Mathey's intentions. He completed the arcaded side wing with large windows offering a view of the summer riding grounds, which stretched from the wing to the newly erected scarp wall and Jelení příkop (today a garden terrace). During the restoration of the riding school after the Prussian bombardment in 1757, a new timberwork roof and a joist ceiling were built. The riding school was subsequently turned into a warehouse.

During post-war conversion into an exhibition hall (a project of Professor Pavel Janák 1946-7, completed in 1949), the interior structures were removed, the windows in the side walls were renovated and enlarged, a basement was built and the entry area adapted. The wooden joist ceiling was reconstructed numerous times and for the most part preserved[37].

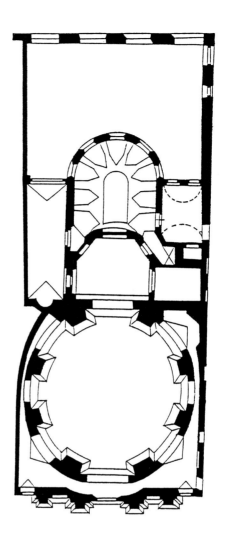

The Church of St Joseph
Malá Strana (The Lesser Quarter)

After the completion of the structure of the Barefooted Carmelites' Cloister, the foundation stone was laid on September 9, 1673 for the Church of St Joseph. The original location of the sanctuary, the first project design and the name of the designer are not known (perhaps P. Dominicus and St Trinità in Rome). A lost dispute with their neighbour, Prince Lobkovic, forced the Carmelites to change the second project design and the location of the church. The abandoned concept, preserved in the form of a copy, can be attributed to Jean-Baptiste Mathey, since evidence exists that he was

involved in the design (a letter written by Count Václav Vojtěch of Šternberk). Mathey located the central simple structure, representing a cross, on a site adjoining the street.

In 1687-1693, after Mathey's concept had been abandoned, the church was built according to the design of Abraham Paris, who was probably not familiar with the local conditions. An adaptation of the original plan was executed by a builder of the Carmelite Order (perhaps Fra Donat Ignaz a Jesu). An inventive façade, with distinct Dutch features, was added. It had to be adapted to the central structure, because the façade was too wide. Several details of the alterations (on the first storey) make it evident that the front and the central part behind it were built as two separate projects and linked

together[38]. The drawing of the left variation published by Hubala is closest to its present day appearance. The interior is of outstanding quality – marble paving from 1711, oak pews of the same date, altars of St Tecla of 1695-96 and St Theresa of 1697 by Matěj Václav Jäckel[39].

Above: Church of St Joseph, ground floor plan and plan at the level of the 1st-floor gallery
Page 193: Church of St Joseph, view

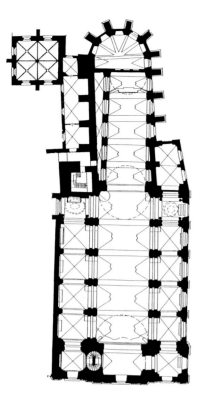

Above: The Church of St James, plan

Above centre: Interior

Above right: Engraving dated c. 1769 (from Huber's Orthography)

Page 195: Panoramic view

The Church of St James
Staré Město (The Old Town)

Evidence of the existence of an early Gothic or Romanesque predecessor of the Baroque church is still unclear. A Minorite church was founded on this site by King Václav (Wenceslas) I in 1232 and consecrated in 1244. The High Gothic remodelling of the monastery with a cross corridor, including a reconstruction of the church, was executed in several phases from the beginning of the 14th century until 1374, when the church was completed and consecrated. Oldřich Avostalis participated in rebuilding it in the Renaissance style after 1581. In 1689 the church and monastery were destroyed by fire, then restored in 1702 under the leadership of architect Jan Šimon Pánek, with the participation of Ottavio Mosto who executed the sculpted decoration of the façade in 1695. The vault surmounting the nave was finished in 1698. Not until a further adaptation was undertaken in 1735-39 was the church interior furnished with the conspicuously colourful decorative elements (stucco lustro by Kristián Schartzmann, stuccowork by Abondio Bolla), and the vault covered with frescoes by František M. Voget.

The organ was built by A. Storck of Loket around 1702. The altars are a magnificent example of the woodwork and decorative craftsmanship of the first half of the 18th century.

The Church of St Margaret and the Benedictine Monastery
Břevnov

The legendary founders of the Břevnov monastery (in 993) were Bishop Vojtěch (Adalbert) of the Slavník family, and the Přemyslid Prince Boleslav II. The origins of its stone Romanesque successor are associated with the personages of Abbot Menhart and a hermit called Vintíř, who was buried there in 1045. The most outstanding relic of that period is the crypt of the monastery church, with remnants of the quadrangle and a circular lavatory. The Romanesque lavatory together with other parts of the original monastery were restored under Abbot Bavor II of Nečtiny, in 1296-1306[40]. This was probably also the date of origin of the core of the Vojtěška, a hexagonal vault over the well. The Hussites turned the monastery into a ruin, which it remained for nearly two hundred years. The church was used only occasionally. A new convent was not built until the second half of the 17th century, under Abbot Sartorius. A truly radical reconstruction of the entire complex took place under the enterprising Abbot Otmar Zinke[41]. The present-day appearance of the church is the outcome of a Baroque restyling, for which the foundation stone was laid in 1708. The authorship of this extremely demanding structure was disputed for many years. Of all the probable authors, Kryštof Dientzenhofer is the most likely.

Kryštof Dientzenhofer, who is also mentioned as the church builder in the diary (or time book) of the construction, which dates from 1709, and who received annual remuneration from the monastery, was preceded by designer Pavel Ignác Bayer, the author of a signed plan of variations (dating from 1702) which were not executed.

The western part of the church, as far as the presbytery, was consecrated in 1712, although intensive work on the choir did not start until 1714 (replacing the choir of the previous sanctuary). The tower was finished in 1715, when the completed western wing of the monastery was also consecrated. The whole of the interior decoration was finished in 1721. The priory was finished in the same year[42].

The extraordinary plasticity of the church architecture is achieved by means of the intersection of vertical cylinders; intersections in the vaulting are marked by the curvilinear edges. Only sections remain from these basic cylinders in the pillars, with neutral fields of the window walls in between. The composition of the intersections in the interior is not quite projected to the outer shell of the structure, which is covered with a neutral flat wall. The interior cylinder is distinct only in the entrance and at the point of contact of the nave with the presbytery. The church, together with the monastery, the landscaped garden and two gateways, represents an architectural complex to which further contributions were subsequently made by a number of masters, including Kilián Ignác Dientzenhofer, Matěj Václav Jäckel, Petr Brandl, Jan Jakub Steinfels, Cosmas Damian Asam and others, until as recently as the 18th century. The first phase of the latest restoration project was completed on the occasion of the millennial anniversary of the monastery existence in 1993[43].

Page 196: The Church of St Margaret, lateral view
Above: Interior

The Church of St Nicholas
Malá Strana (The Lesser Quarter)

The origins of the church are connected with the
redesign of the entire centre of Lesser Quarter Square[44].
The foundation stone was laid on September 6 1673,
together with the foundation of the front wall, which
was brought up to ground floor level by 1674. The
builder, P. Bos, proceeded according to a plan based
either on variations of an earlier date (drawn up in 1672
with the involvement of D. Orsi de Orsini), or on a
variation supplied by Francesco Caratti in March 1673.
But the project did not progress any further until a new

contract was concluded in 1676, with G.D. Orsi de
Orsini for continuation of the work, in keeping with
his variation on the plot of land earmarked for the
Monastic House. Meanwhile, the Gothic church was
preserved.

The crucial stage in the development of the church can
be seen in the period after 1702. The spatial and
ground-plan concepts totally changed. They came to be
determined by the intersections of forms and a curvilinear plan. Kryštof Dientzenhofer is generally regarded
as the author of the design, though no direct archival
evidence to this effect exists. The project progressed at
a remarkable speed between 1703 and 1705, so that the
part of the nave adjacent to the front was roofed as

early as 1705 and surmounted with a vault in 1709. Kryštof Dientzenhofer is only mentioned as one of the expert advisers in the assessment of the old Gothic tower. The Gothic church stayed in its place until 1711, when a part of the new church (the entrance and two traverses of the vault) was brought to such an advanced state that it could be used for worship. A plan dated 1727[45], which coincides with the plan found in the Groensteyn-Kiedrich archive, clearly documents what was previously proved by photogrammetric analysis[46] – namely that the third vault traverse, and in fact the entire structure from the line behind the pillars of the second travee onwards, had not been built until Kryštof Dientzenhofer's son Kilián Ignác took

over the work. Further arguments in favour of this assumption are Werner's view of the unfinished nave, and the results from the above-mentioned photogrammetric analysis of the contour lines of the nave vaulting (a different technique was used for the vaulting of the third field, without the insertion of oval windows). The church was temporarily enclosed by a wall with an illusory painted altar. The oval All Souls' Chapel (or Chapel of the Deceased) was finished in 1713, and the opposite Chapel of St Anne in 1715. In 1737, the municipality requested and achieved the resumption of construction work under the leadership of, and according to a new project by, Kilián Ignác Dientzenhofer. Whatever was left of the Gothic church had been

removed by 1743. By 1745 the walls had been erected up to the level of the entablature and the cornices. In 1750 a board of experts dispelled public fears of a collapse of the unprecedentedly complex structure. In 1751, the dome with a temporary roof was erected, to be covered a year later with copper plates. A dispute regarding the ownership of the tower was won by the municipality. The existence of a model of the tower, which, however, has not been preserved, is mentioned. The tower was, in essence, finished as early as 1752, and later alterations by Anselmo Lurago are therefore insignificant. After the Prussian bombardment in 1752, which gravely damaged the church exterior, work continued on the interior. The compass windows in the

old part of the vault were bricked up, the bands in the older two travees were then probably cut off, and the vault assumed the character of a vaguely undulating surface.

The fresco on the nave vault, showing a scene from the life of St Nicholas, was painted in 1760 by Jan Lukas Kracker. The organ was built in 1745-46 by Tomáš Schwartz. The giant figures of the saints on the pillars in the nave and the crossing are the work of Ignác Platzer (1755-69), and so is the copper statue on the main altar. The photographs also show the frescoes of Jan Hager and Josef Redelmayer above the tribunes, and the fresco in the cupola by František X.K. Palko.

Above left: St Nicholas, 2nd quarter of the 18th century
(Engraving by B.B. Werner)
Above: Panoramic view

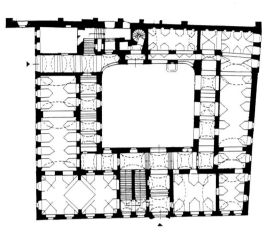

Former Jesuit School
Malá Strana (The Lesser Quarter)

A project of high architectural quality involving Baroque remodelling of a large complex of buildings grouped around two courtyards, and forming a large portion of the northern wall of Lesser Quarter Square, resulted in full stylistic unity of the entire eastern part around the entrance courtyard. The western wing, around the second courtyard, with Gothic parcelling, and Renaissance and Baroque, as well as modern alterations, represents a mixture of these stages without major artistic value.

The eastern part, which underwent three Baroque remodellings, bears an imprint of the grand concept adopted by the Jesuits in the 18th century. A 17th-century early Baroque adaptation of the southeastern corner, an older Renaissance structure and a Gothic basement were absorbed by a second Baroque redesign in 1709-11. This older part can still be analysed today in the southeastern corner. In other parts, however, the

structure registered under land registry number 1 is of a later date (1724-26), and respects new street lines. An extant plan, drawn by Kilián Ignác Dientzenhofer in 1727[47], determines the author of the reconstruction, which included the most complicated and multiform portal of the High Baroque period in Prague.

It can only be guessed to what degree the author borrowed the shapes and concept of the façade and the monumental stairway from the author of the older reconstruction (who, according to our hypothesis, was Kryštof Dientzenhofer).

This remarkably extensive structure, situated at such an important place in the city, was altered several times afterwards (1784-89 by architect Tomáš Haffenecker, and in 1808-1830). The third storey was erected over the western wing in 1845. In 1850 the house was made the seat of the Vice-Regent, and after World War I it was assigned to the Land Authority. These changes in use brought about further alterations, especially in the interiors – for instance in the conference hall[48].

Above, from left to right: Jesuit School, c. 1769 (Engraving by Huber); portal; ground floor plan

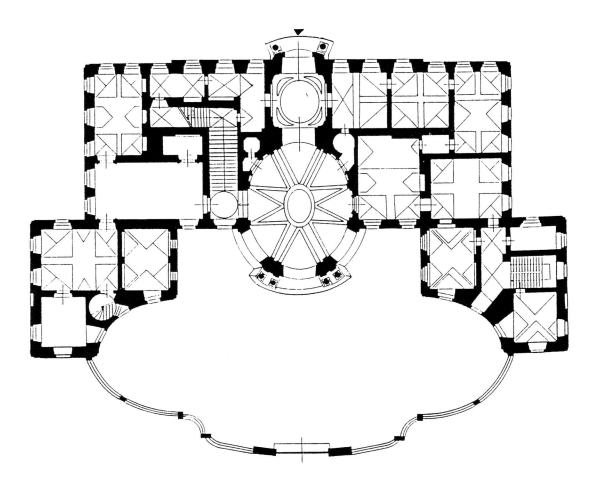

Lobkovic Palace
Malá Strana (The Lesser Quarter)

In the same way as the Thun Palace, the Lobkovic Palace originated as a completely new structure, without making use of the older buildings which existed on this site as early as the Middle Ages (i.e. the Strahov brewery).

Interpretation is made difficult by the fact that the archive of the Přehořovsky family has not been preserved. In 1696, Count František Karel started purchasing the gardens. A record of the purchase was entered in the land register in 1702, and the building permit for the palace was issued in the same year. Both Franz and Preiss refer to Schaller's information about the start of the construction in 1703. According to the testimony of the builders Antonio Lurago and Kryštof

Dientzenhofer, dated April 24, 1704, in Count K. Přehořovsky's dispute concerning water conduit, the palace was newly built. But that probably involved only the basic structure, because such speed of construction is improbable. The date of 1707, seems more likely[49]. Though the entry in the land register may not directly relate to the construction project, according to Plachta there is already evidence of the palace's existence in 1708. The interior decoration took the craftsmen another few years to finish[50] (Tomáš Soldati 1710, stonemason Pietro della Torre). In 1713 the palace was sold; in 1769 it was damaged by fire; another storey was added in 1767, probably by architect Ignác Palliardi. Its original appearance can be seen in a drawing by Werner.

The noteworthy composition – an oval cylinder inserted into the undulating front facing towards the garden, with the adjacent entry vestibule, the upper-storey hall

and the elegant stairway entered from the open vestibule – is characterized by an ornamental plan and refined form. Kubíček and Naňková ascribed the palace to architect Giovanni Battista Alliprandi from a comparative analysis of other structures designed by him. We share their opinion. Literature also suggests Jan Blažej (Giovanni) Santini (Franz) and Domenico Martinelli (Birnbaumová) as potential authors.

Above: Lobkovic Palace, ground floor plan
Page 203, top: Lobkovic Palace, 2nd quarter of the 18th century (Engraving by B.B. Werner)
Page 203, bottom: Panoramic view

Thun (Kolovrat) Palace
Malá Strana (The Lesser Quarter)

Though this palace ranks among the most representative works of Czech Baroque architecture, the history of the process which ultimately resulted in its present appearance is not clear from archive documents. Research[51] has nonetheless proved beyond doubt that the palace was built as a new structure from the basement to the roof (with the exception of the western peripheral wall). This is a rare phenomenon in the Prague environment, where remodelled and adapted buildings predominate.

The site was built up as early as the 13th century. The present-day Neruda Street has always served as one of the traffic arteries leading out of the city. Since the construction of the new palace did away with older structures, we shall not concern ourselves with the Gothic, Renaissance and early Baroque stages. It should be noted that new construction of the palace in the early Baroque style after 1688, attributed to a design by Domenico Orsini, is highly improbable (G.D. Orsi died in 1679). An old Renaissance house of the Slavata family stretched through the whole site from the Old Castle Stairs as far as Neruda Street. It is still fully preserved in its Renaissance form in the northern half of the site. The southern portion of the former Slavata Palace (now the Thun Palace) obviously would not have been pulled down in the 1820's if it had been newly built.

The idea of building a new palace (in place of the one they acquired in 1693) was conceived by the new owners, the Libštejns of Kolovraty, in 1708. They engaged in complicated negotiations with their neighbours – the Theatine Convent – and finally reached an agreement. Since it is assumed that the designer of the reconstruction of the Theatine church was Jan Blažej Santini, this link cannot be disregarded when inquiring about the palace architect. Because Santini also worked for the Kolovrat family in Rychnov nad Kněžnou, and as analysis of the structural composition supports the hypothesis of Santini's authorship, most researchers agree, with a high degree of justification, that he was the palace architect. This is our view, too. The Thun Palace is impressive for its advanced composition of shapes, dating to the period after 1709 – or 1716. The massive sculptural architecture of the block, with the prominent motifs of the entry portal embellished with the Kolovrat Eagle emblems, and a series of perfect details (richly profiled cornices above the windows, the base, the crown cornice, the three-nave and two-column entry vestibule), was created in collaboration with Matthias Braun (judging from the results of style analysis, though archive evidence is not available). On the whole, the palace has been preserved up to the present in its original form – only individual parts have been altered. In 1791 the builder Jos. Zobel adapted the stairway. Further major adaptations were made in 1828, 1844 and 1852, involving partial modernization of the interiors. In 1869, a whole pleiad of artists – whose names are associated with the interior decoration of the National Theatre in Prague (J. Tulka, F. Ženíšek, A. Levy, J. Scheiwl and J. Trenkwald) worked here under the leadership of architect Josef Zítek on the decoration of the redesigned main stairway. It was at this time that the neo-Renaissance details were added (i.e. the doors, windows, decoration of the interior). Rising from the northern side of the spacious courtyard is the massive wall of the Slavata Palace, adapted in 1846-47 by the builder J. Bělsky. The palace wing of the Thun Palace facing Neruda Street is but a part of the extensive layout (now the Italian Embassy) which, in the western portion towards the Castle Stairs, has retained the Renaissance appearance of the Slavata House.

Above left: Thun Palace, 2nd quarter of the 18th century
(Engraving by B.B. Werner)
Above right: Façade
Page 205: Portal

The Church of the Holy Trinity
Nové Město (The New Town)

The layout of the structure is symbolic; the Holy Trinity is symbolized by means of three spatial fields, surmounted by Bohemian vaulting and cross vaults with lunettes. The triple division permeates both the front entrance and the side façades, as well as their vertical extension, which has a central cupola on a tambour, topped with a central tower. The structure was erected between 1708 and 1712, and was consecrated in 1713. The Trinitarian Order, however, first considered the project in 1705, (the permission to build a monastery was granted to the Trinitarians after they had been active in Prague for two years, in a temporary facility at the Na Slupi location).

Of considerable significance are two contracts concluded on August 17, 1708. The second of them in particular, signed by Count Putz, Ottavio Broggio, Jan Jiří Aichbauer and his foster father Kryštof Dientzenhofer,

is important not only in view of the construction project itself but also for determining the role played by Kryštof Dientzenhofer in this case. K. Dientzenhofer himself, as head of the family business, and Aichbauer pledged under the contract to build the church according to the plans of architect Ottavio Broggio from Litoměřice. Thus, Kryštof Dientzenhofer had the status of executive builder implementing the ideas of another architect. Responsibility for the project was later assumed by Jan Jiří Aichbauer, according to two amendments dated 1710 and 1711 concerning the building of the central tower and the cupola.

According to a chronogram on the façade, the construction was completed in 1712, when a contract was concluded with Aichbauer for furnishing the interior. The Trinitarian monastery, its axis a follow-on of the church, was built subsequently[52].

The church underwent a series of alterations; the choir was remodelled after 1740, the frescoes on the vault were executed by A. Schlachter in 1779, the interior was adapted in 1778-80[53]. The monastery was abolished

in 1783 and turned into barracks, which were pulled down in the late 19th century. The church was repaired in 1879, 1896, and in 1991 when the façade was repainted (the choice of the colour scheme is rather controversial).

The remarkable central composition with the symbolism of the number three (the Holy Trinity) catches the eye thanks to the uplifting effect produced by the lighting of the interior and the high-quality profiling of the composite orders. The pilasters have typical edges 'drawn in' on the diagonal of the supporting structure, producing an optically slimming effect. A collection of plans by Ottavio Broggio has been published[54].

Above: The Church of the Holy Trinity, façade
Page 207: The Church of the Holy Trinity, original designs, Ott. Broggio, after 1708

207

The Church of St John of Nepomuk
Hradčany (The Castle)

The Church of St John of Nepomuk is a superb example of the composition skills of architect Kilián Ignác Dientzenhofer, whose creation is characterized by an extraordinarily fine sense of harmony between works of architecture and their setting. Even though only its shell survived the demolition of the structure in 1836, the original layout can still be appreciated today; it is evident on Langweil's model.

The church construction started in 1720 under the leadership of architect Kryštof Dientzenhofer. The design of the structure that we know today had an antecedent. The plan has been preserved, but this building was never executed, and is rather conservative compared to the design of K. Dientzenhofer's other projects. It is also interesting to note that the name of architect Jeronymus Costa[57], until then less well-known, is mentioned on the commemorative plaque installed at the time of the church foundation.

(He is also mentioned as the architect of other, high-quality compositions of that time – e.g. Manětín). Kryštof Dientzenhofer died in 1722, but from 1716, the business was gradually taken over – according to the documentation of contemporary projects – by his son Kilián Ignác, then about thirty years old. He was a talented, experienced man, who definitely had a say in the projects executed by his father.

Therefore, we assume that the author of the neoclassical central composition, and also the author of the dynamic additional vestibule and the precise composition of the portal was Kilián Ignác Dientzenhofer. The clear layout of the front, the boldness of the structure (the vault over the central part – adapted Bohemian vault, the huge window in the front), the fine detail, and the sober décor testify to the authorship of this master of Prague Baroque architecture. The construction was protracted until 1728, and the church was not consecrated until August 21 1729.

A superb feature of the interior is the fresco by Václav Vavřinec Reiner, depicting a scene from the life of St John of Nepomuk. The church composition is closely linked with that of the 'imperial hospital', situated towards the north (also designed by Kilián Ignác Dientzenhofer), and the former Ursuline Convent in the south. The church and convent were however abolished in 1786, and the church equipment was sold at an auction in the 1760s[58].

The quality of the church has never been disputed, although it was used for a long time as a storage place and later on as a garrison church. This was the reason why its façade and plan are included in the so-called 'Jäger's Copybook'. Thanks to this, the helm roof of the tower could be restored after it had been removed in the 1930s and replaced with a simple tent-like structure. The helm roof project was completed in 1993, together with a repair of the façade.

Above left: The Church of St John of Nepomuk, façade
Above right: Imperial Hospital, façade
Page 209: The Church of St John of Nepomuk, interior

The church composition also includes the adjacent walls and the stairways, which form a cosy miniature 'cour d'honneur'. In 1836 the house 'U černého mouřenína' ('The Pitch-black Moor House') was pulled down, and an illusive wall, complementing the opposite wall of the hospital, was added in the north by Kilián Ignác Dientzenhofer.

Above left: Ground floor plan and Below-vault level plan
Above, centre and right: Original designs by Kilián Ignác Dientzenhofer

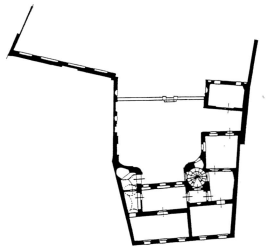

The House of Heinrich Dientzenhofer
Malá Strana (The Lesser Quarter, Všehrdova Street)

The house stood on a site surrounded by gardens, on the outskirts of the city near the Baroque ramparts. Parts of the ground floor were preserved from a Renaissance structure of an earlier date. The reconstruction in 1725 avoided this core, to the right of the entry, and through a difficult layout incorporated it into the structure.

A major landmark in the architectural history of the house was its sale in 1725 to Heinrich Dientzenhofer (brother of the architect Kilián Ignác) and its subsequent reconstruction, documented in a record made by the Visitation Commission in 1725, and by Merhaut's information quoting a source which is missing today.

In 1730, Kilián Ignác Dientzenhofer confirmed that the house was ramshackle, and that he therefore built a new one in its place from lime and stone. An inland revenue inspector of that time described the façade as beautiful[55]. Today the house is in a deplorable state of repair.

In 1844, the street façade was reworked. In 1811 and in 1905 a small courtyard gallery with segments into the cross beams was added.

The façade, regarded as beautiful in the first quarter of the 18th century, is now lost, and the courtyard façade damaged. Yet it is obvious that the house was designed ingeniously in terms of its composition. Today we can admire only the façade facing the garden and remnants of the architectural composition of the enclosing walls. Judging by an indication on Langweil's model of Prague, and by the remains of the architectural articulation seen on site, it can be noted that the cosy garden became an important part of the overall composition. It was decorated with illusory frescoes on the walls, niches of a rhythmic quality, and architectural motifs. An interesting feature is the use of roughcast walls, structured by means of crenellated diagonal brick bonding.

This modestly sized structure documents its author's extraordinary skills, which allowed him to create a masterpiece even on a small scale, with the garden and the house representing a coherent harmonious whole. The mentality of a grand, dynamic Baroque style is presented here in miniature form[56].

Above left: The House of Heinrich Dientzenhofer, garden façade
Above: 1st-floor plan

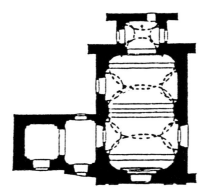

The Convent of the Order of St Elizabeth
Nové Město (The New Town)

The whole complex was restyled, with new structures built in place of older ones in 1724-62, mostly by Kilián Ignác Dientzenhofer. It comprises the convent (1726-27), the Church of Our Lady of Sorrow (1724-25) and a hospital (1728-41). The portion with the Chapel of St Thecla was rebuilt in 1761-62. A cross made in 1738 was placed in front of it. The latest redesign of the terrain took place in 1904, when the surface level of the roadway of Na Slupi Street was lowered.

The longitudinal church consists of two vault fields surmounted with Bohemian vaulting, and a narrower, oblong rather than square, presbytery. Pilasters form the tectonically active elements of the interior, contrasting with the flat, unbroken surface of the walls. The exterior displays a loose pattern of sensitive variegation. The intended project of building a convent of the Celestine Order on the opposite site would have resulted in an interesting complex, but never materialized due to the intolerance of the Order of St Elizabeth. The plans of architect Kilián Ignác Dientzenhofer for the Celestine convent have been preserved[60].

Top: The Church of Our Lady of Sorrow, plan
Above left: The Convent of the Order of St Elizabeth
Above: The Convent of the Order of St Elizabeth, 2nd quarter of the 18th century (Engraving by B.B. Werner)

The Church of St Thomas
Malá Strana (The Lesser Quarter)

The Order of the Augustinian Hermits came to Prague in 1285. The church and monastery were founded by King Václav (Wenceslas) II on a site that was probably originally occupied by the older building of the Church and Chapel of St Dorothea. The church remodelling took place in the 14th century (the presbytery was finished in 1315, the three-nave structure after the first half of the 14th century, the church was consecrated in 1379). In 1420 it was burnt out, and again damaged by fire in 1541. A new vault was built in 1552. The church was rebuilt between 1584 and 1592, probably according to the plans of Bernardo di Alberto; it was vaulted over, and the new northern tower was finished. The portal, completed after 1623, was carved by stonemason Campioni de Bossi, as documented by a contract of

1617[59]. In 1723, the church tower and vault were damaged by lightning. During restoration in 1725-1731, architect Kilián Ignác Dientzenhofer provided the main nave with a new vault, the dome was built, and the vaulting of the presbytery completed (a detailed budget of the construction project was drawn by Kilián Ignác Dientzenhofer in 1727). The massive, dynamic front was designed so as to contrast with the prismatoid tower of an earlier date. The ceiling frescoes in the nave were painted by Václav Vavřinec Reiner in 1828-30. The nave was consecrated in 1729, the presbytery in 1731. The impressive sculptural composition of the western façade is not an end in itself; the protruding pillars and columns reinforce the walls which started coming apart. The façade is best appreciated when viewed from below at a steep angle, or obliquely from Lesser Quarter Square, as was the designer's intent. The massive side portal concludes the vista through Josefská Street, as its focal point. The slender tower fits

well into the panorama of The Lesser Quarter, and together with the tower and dome of the Church of St Nicholas, built later, forms its primary landmark.

Above, from left to right: The Church of St Thomas, interior; façade; panorama

213

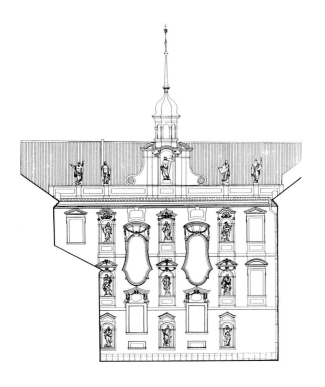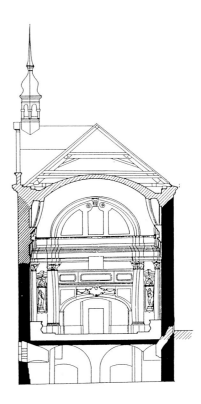

The Church of St Bartholomew
Staré Město (The Old Town)

The site was already built up in the Middle Ages. At the initiative of the Czech preacher and reformer Jan Milíč of Kroměříž, several houses of dubious repute were pulled down and replaced with a building called 'Jerusalem' (a monastery with a chapel). At some time after 1660 it was converted into a church by the Jesuits, and in 1678 the structure was damaged by fire. Between 1726 and 1731, architect Kilián Ignác Dientzenhofer rebuilt an older structure, building new vaults supported with added pillars over the partly preserved peripheral walls; the basement pillars were reinforced at the same time. The interior, based on a curvilinear plan, and the exterior are dualistically composed. Of extraordinary importance is the treatment of the northern façade facing towards the courtyard between the 'Konvikt' building (in the construction of which both Dientzenhofers participated, too) and the older structure of the Convent of the Order of Grey Sisters

(probably built according to the plan of architect Jean-Baptiste Mathey in the 1670s).

The northern wall of the church, of which the lower three quarters date back to the Gothic period with post-Gothic additions, was restyled as a coulisse of the courtyard. In relation to the interior, the front is shifted by half a module; the chasuble-shaped interior and exterior windows were provided with dividers permitting separate symmetrical treatment of the exterior and the interior. In the side traverses, the structural solution of the traverses of the prior building, designed by Jean-Baptiste Mathey, was included in the composition[61].

Kilián Ignác Dientzenhofer thus applied his supreme talent to achieve effective incorporation of the structure into its surroundings, making use of older substructures. The result was a distinctive, inimitable composition. The courtyard façade is richly decorated in the niches and on the attic with statues by a hitherto unidentified sculptor.

The façade in Bartolomějská Street is very simple. Kilián Ignác Dientzenhofer seems to have borrowed the

motif of ventilation windows from an older, early Baroque structure. 'Jäger's Copybook' indicates the original intention regarding the way the façade was to be diversified. The frescoes on the Bohemian vault in the church interior were painted by Václav Vavřinec Reiner around 1731; they depict the martyrdom of St Bartholomew, the Virgin Mary and St John of Nepomuk. A portrait of Bishop Daniel Mayer can be seen above the choir[62].

Above, from left to right: The Church of St Bartholomew, façade viewed from the courdyard; longitudinal section; cross-section
Page 215: The Church of St Bartholomew, interior

The House 'U zlatého jelena' ('At the Golden Deer')
Malá Strana (The Lesser Quarter, Tomášská Street)

The façade from the High Baroque period conceals an older Renaissance house, built on land sold by the monastery at the end of the 16th century. The Renaissance house was narrower. The early Baroque character of its peripheral and inner walls, and the out-come of their substantial reconstruction during the High Baroque period have remained preserved. Mádl's argument in favour of the probable authorship of architect Kilián Ignác Dientzenhofer, with Ferdinand Maximilian Brokoff as his collaborator, has withstood both further research in the archives and the compilation of SURPMO reports. The noble design, displaying motifs analogous to those found on other structures designed by this architect, and the direct relation with the construction of the Church of St Thomas, which took place at the same time (and on which he collabo-rated with Brokoff), testify to Kilián Ignác Dientzenhofer as the author, too. The preparation of the reconstruction is documented by an agreement concluded by the property owner, Kašpar Fridrich, with his neighbour in 1723, and Fridrich's request, addressed in 1725, to the Prior of the Monastery of St Thomas, stating that the owner 'fundamentally' renovated the house[63].

Above: 'U zlatého jelena', façade

The house 'U modré lišky' ('At the Blue Fox')
Malá Strana (The Lesser Quarter, Kampa Island)

The single-storey corner house with a built-in attic concludes the whole of the western side of the lovely Na Kampě square (on Kampa Island). This characteristic Prague house with a simple hexaxial façade has framed windows with the typical detail of guttae on the side protrusions of the upper portion of the portal.

The very simple plaster stucco façade is embellished with a charming house-sign above the main door. The date '1664' is carved into the beam above the threshold. Two cartouches are lined with volutes, acanthi with flowers, clouds and heads of cherubs. The house-sign of a fox holding a twig in its mouth, executed in bas-relief and framed by the lower cartouche, gave the house its name.

The house was built soon after 1605. Of the original structure, the basic sub-structures of the ground floor and part of the vaulting have survived. Most of the first storey was restyled in the Baroque period (1664). The

attic already existed, according to Huber's orthography, in the first half of the 18th century. The present-day stairway was built in 1810.

The handsome asymmetrical composition of this small Lesser Quarter house testifies to the sensitivity of the approach taken by its anonymous Baroque builders and plasterers.

Above: 'U modré lišky'

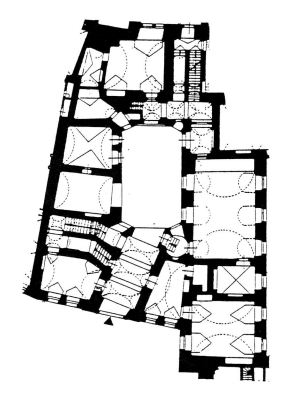

Above: The Maltese Convent, plan and view

The Maltese Convent
Malá Strana (The Lesser Quarter)

The structure is an example of the mastery of the architect. His skill is evident in the way he incorporates the regular oblong courtyard and the clear layout, a passageway running askew, a cleverly situated stairway, and the regular rhythm of the façade into the irregular site – with maximum use of older walls (of which the adjacent one is of the ashlar Romanesque type). The convent was probably built by architect Tomáš Haffenecker in 1728-31. It was not finished until after his death (in 1730). The new building of the convent was furnished with high quality Baroque joinery details (Ondřej Bullow, the doors, gate, windows and floors). The metal fittings on them were executed by blacksmiths J.J. Wolff and J.J. Scheib.

The Convent of the Order of Maltese Knights has always been interconnected with the neighbouring Church of Our Lady Below the Chain, and is related to it in terms of the structural characteristics and layout[64].

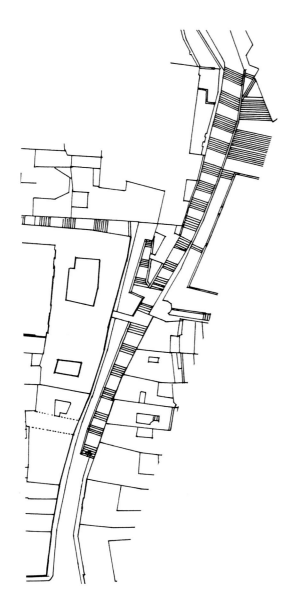

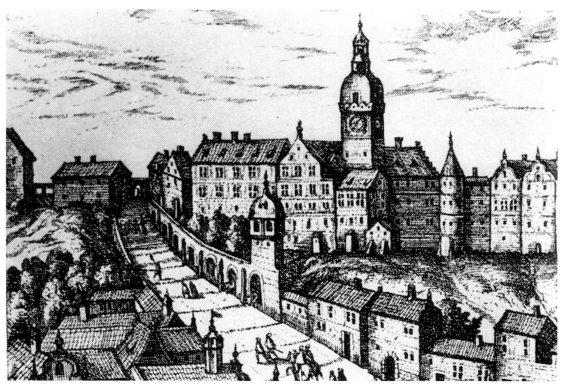

The New Castle Stairs
Malá Strana (The Lesser Quarter)

The stairs connect Lesser Quarter Square with Hradčanské (Castle) Square. They were built in the 16th century. The enclosing wall of the castle garden, which they adjoin, is mostly of Renaissance origin, but was adapted when the garden bower was built for Emperor Matthias in 1614, and again in 1722. Sculptures by Ferdinand Maximilian Brokoff were to be installed in the niches at that time, as a parallel to the decoration of Charles Bridge.

Above left: The New Castle Stairs, layout

Above: 18th century engraving

Right: Panorama

Archbishop's Palace
Hradčany

The extensive structure, occupying a whole block, stands in a place of honour, in close proximity to Prague Castle and on the access route to it. Its basic appearance is influenced by that of its Renaissance predecessor, a house built by Florián Gryspek in 1538. A devastating fire in 1541, became the stimulus for the conversion of the palace into a Renaissance seat of a high-ranking state official. In 1561, when the Prague archbishopric was reinstated, the palace was bought by Emperor Ferdinand I, with the intention of making it the seat of the archbishop. Ferdinand I donated it to the new Archbishop Antonín Brus of Mohelnice. Alterations were made in 1561 and 1562 by Jan Tyrol. The detailed construction project was further elaborated by Bonifác Wohlmuth or Jan Tyrol. The Renaissance palace occupied the same area of land as the present-day structure (except for the uniaxial lateral additions made at a later date). As with the Schwarzenberg Palace standing opposite, it had a lunette cornice with sgraffito decoration by a painter called Florián. The sgraffito is still preserved on the courtyard façade[65]. The palace chapel on the first floor was built at the end of the 16th century, and decorated with stucco-work and frescoes by Daniel Alexius of Květná. Its remodelling in 1676-79 was led by the new architect Jean-Baptiste Mathey, whom the archbishop brought from Rome. Mathey designed the palace in the style of Roman Vignolian academism, which still represents the basis of the present day composition of the main wing, even in detail. Mathey designed the new marble portal with a balcony, and situated the stairway where it can be found today. The contemporary appearance of the palace can be seen in Werner's engraving and in a sketch kept in the collections of the Strahov Library. The diversification of Mathey's façade is still observable on the stairway part of the façade. The palace was restyled once more in the 18th century, according to the design of de Oliva (the project was led by Pavel Ignác Bayer in 1722-25). But the palace did not assume its present-day appearance until the time of architect J. Wirth[66]. He finalized its architectural development in 1764-65, above all by adding short wings with oval parlours, designing the Rococo ornamentation of the façade, adapting the vestibule and the stairway, and creating the courtyard using a majestic gallery to partition the existing deep space. He did, however, leave the marble portal of 1676 and the stone window jambs in place, as outstanding elements of the composition and the Rococo façade.

Above: Archbishop's Palace, chapel

Page 221, above: Ground floor plan

Page 221, bottom: Procession at the occasion of the coronation of Leopold II, 1791 (Engraving by Cash. Pluth)

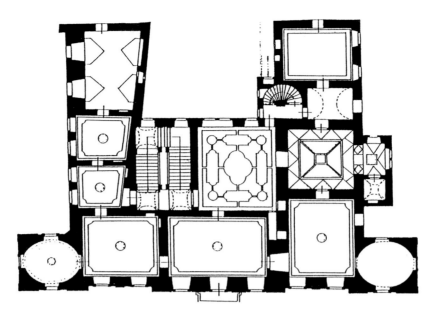

Abovet: Vyšehrad Fortifications, 1680-85 (Detail from a panoramic view of Prague, engraving by Folpertus van Ouden-Allen)
Above right: Vyšehrad Fortifications

Vyšehrad Fortifications

Following several proposals for the fortification of Prague, and the execution of some minor fortification works at the beginning of the Thirty Years War, a plan was produced for the city defences, based on the concept of General Raimund Montecuccoli. He intended to change Prague into a fortress with two citadels – one to be built at Strahov or at Prague Castle, and the other at Vyšehrad. Documentation for the construction of the Vyšehrad fort was supplied in 1650 by

Colonel Inocenc de Conti. Giuseppe Priami, charged with supervision of the construction project, proposed several amendments of the fortification system, the construction of which was under way by then. The construction was executed by Carlo Lurago and others. The defence system with corner bastions, stuck-out ramparts and gates, soon proved to be obsolete, and its shortcomings became fully evident in 1741 and 1744, even before it was finished. The fortifications added to the architecture of Prague massive cubes of roughcast brick walls, armoured at the corners with sandstone ashlars[77].

The Vrtba Garden

The Vrtba Palace was built gradually, growing in a complicated organic way in front of the Újezd Gate. A Gothic wine press still forms a part of the northern wing. The front building was purchased in 1580 by A. Avostalis and improved by him. In 1631 both houses were interconnected in a utilitarian Baroque reconstruction project[75]. Documents on further reconstruction, led by Kryštof Dientzenhofer as the executing contractor, relate to the year 1713. A newly built

structure is already referred to at the end of 1715, and in 1716. Records on costs incurred in erecting the new structure of the sala terrena are dated 1716. It is regarded as probable that this project, too, was led by Kryštof Dientzenhofer. Rochus Bolla is mentioned in 1718, as the plasterer. Since František Maximilián Kaňka was employed as an architect by the family of the Counts of Vrtba, his involvement in designing the garden is not ruled out, even though this assumption does not rely on any archive evidence[76].

Above: The Vrtba Garden, view of the terrace
Page 225, above: The Vrtba Garden, terrace
Page 225, bottom: Stairway

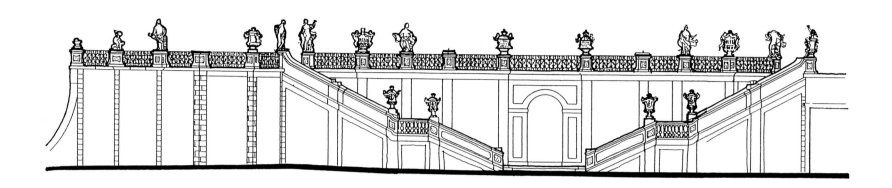

225

The Palace Gardens below Prague Castle
Malá Strana (The Lesser Quarter)

A major motif in the panorama of Prague Castle is the wreath of greenery on the castle hillside. This seemingly compact verdure is actually composed of individual terraced gardens, each of them designed in its own characteristic style, adjoining the palaces in Valdštejnská (Wallenstein) Street and the New Castle Stairs. Because of the steep gradient of the castle hill, terraces with supportive retaining walls, crowned with stone or iron railings and balustrades predominate. They are combined with garden alcoves (arbours) and stairways of ornamental design. Hradčany was originally bare, as was required by the logic of fortified castles; vineyards serving as a strategically important foreground.

The beginning of cultivation on a part of Hradčany – the planting of vineyards by the Monastery of St George – is located by Tomek in the 12th-13th century. In the 15th century the monastery started selling off the individual plots of land to the burghers of The Lesser Quarter. The gardens were given their present day appearance in the 18th and 19th centuries, when they were remodelled in the style of late Baroque and, in part, in the Romantic style. The first garden of major importance – east of Písecká gate, the Brusnice stream and the Vltava flood plain called Na Písku ('On the Sands') – is the Fürstenberg Garden (now the garden of

the Polish Embassy). It occupies nearly one quarter of the palace gardens below Prague Castle. It was founded on land belonging to the former house of Jan Václav Berka of Dubé. It had features of a self-contained Renaissance garden, with a flower garden and an orchard. During the Thirty Years War this part of the area below the castle was 'a ruined, desolate place'. The garden boundaries of the northern portion were altered in 1674, when the 'Old Castle Stairs' were built on a new scarp and enclosing walls.

The palace was remodelled in Baroque style in two stages (after 1714, by Václav Albrecht of Vrbno and Freudenthal; and after 1743, when it was acquired by Václav Kazimír Netolicky of Eisenberg, who bought – together with the palace – the garden with a small house in it, the vineyard and a wine press[67]). We assume that the Baroque alteration of the garden took place in the second stage. The resultant composition is captured, in an abbreviated form, in Huber's panorama of 1679, and is documented by Herget's measurements of 1790. The garden pavilion at the conclusion of the great architectural axis, with a partly preserved stairway, was probably built closely after 1790 by architect I.F. Palliardi, who also designed the arbour of the Černín Palace garden at about the same time. In 1820, Karel Egon, Prince of Fürstenberg, decided to build a timber store and iron warehouse in the lower flat part for storing the products of his steel mill in Nižbor. The garden underwent a major change in 1860, when the timber yard was demolished, the Valdštejnská Street

line was changed, and the wall was replaced with a cast-iron fence. The lower part of the garden was restyled as an English park by Liebl, the Prince's garden architect, according to a plan dating from 1859. The outcome of this restyling has survived, with only minor alterations, to the present day.

The neighbouring Černín, or Small Fürstenberg Garden is one of the most charming garden compositions in which the layout and spatial quality of Prague architecture of the late Baroque period found their expression. In conjunction with the reconstruction, in several stages between 1759 and 1776, of the house, the Černíns added the narrow strip of a garden plot that rises steeply in the direction of Prague Castle. In a costly late Baroque restyling for the lower palace of Countess Marie Barbora of Černín, architect Ignác Palliardi, who is believed to have been the author of the entire composition, created the splendid environment, the whole of which shows evidence of architec-

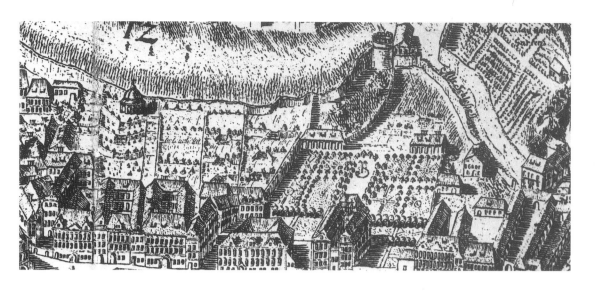

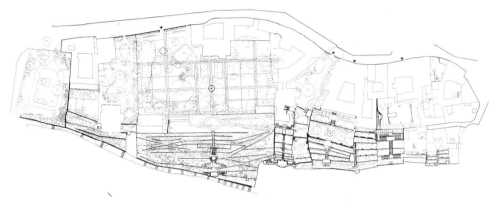

227

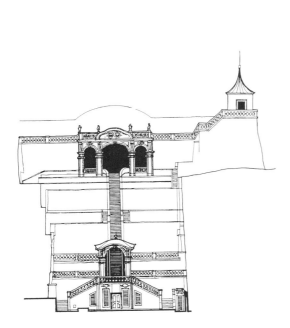
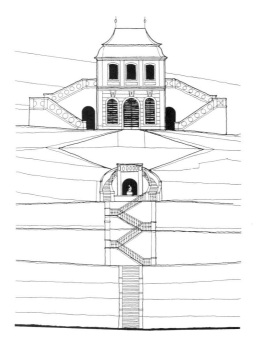
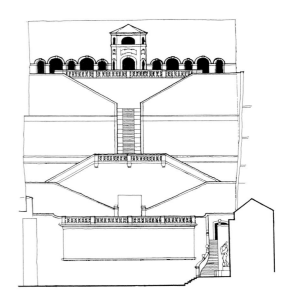

tural treatment. The axial composition, its backbone formed by the practically endless stairway, is lent a rhythmic quality by the open bower, decorative arch and terrace walls with decorative parapets. The whole composition leads to the upper triaxial loggia, with an emblem of the alliance of the Černín and Schaffgotsch families in the cartouche; and even higher to the terrace, which is accessed by means of a staircase of playful design, with a small cylindrical tower. In the first half of the 19th century the garden and the palace were bought by the Fürstenbergs, the owners of the neighbouring palaces (Palffy Palace and Fürstenberg Palace). That is why the garden is also called 'Malá Fürstenberská' ('Small Fürstenberg').

The Palffy Garden has retained a part of its Baroque architectural design, which is still apparent on the stairway and the vista with a sun dial (now a renovated modern version). Its eastern enclosing wall absorbed the Gothic wall of The Lesser Quarter of Prague founded in 1257.

The terraced composition of the Ledebour garden was probably developed on the steep slope of the hill in two stages[68]. The lower part is flat, and directly adjoins the Ledebour palace. It contributes to the demanding design of the rear garden patio, with a sala terrena in the western part, and a coulisse staircase wall, which, by means of a sideways shift of perspective, counterbal-

ances the irregularity of the terrain on the eastern edge of the parcel. The tall terrace wall in the north concludes the space, which has perfect acoustics.

Unravelling the riddle of authorship is extremely difficult, because the vast amount of information leads us in different directions. Thus A. Kubíček ascribed the authorship in 1946, to Jan Blažej Santini. (The Trauttmannsdorfs figured among the debtors to a high amount during the settlement of Santini's assets after his death, and the Zwettel plan for Plasy, too, clearly documents this architect's garden landscaping skills.) In 1973 E. Poche and E. Preiss hypothesized[69,70] that the author was the Trauttmannsdorfs' architect, Giovanni Battista Alliprandi. Macek, Vlček, and Zahradník accept the possibility of the creative participation of František Maximilián Kaňka[71]. The situation is obscured by the fact that Kaňka collaborated with all the above-mentioned architects, or completed their projects. Moreover, soon before the intended execution of the Ledebour Garden (1715-18) Kaňka probably also designed the Vrtba Garden on the opposite slope of Petřín Hill, in collaboration with the contractor firm of Kryštof Dientzenhofer[72,73]. We accept these hypotheses, as well as that of Bašeová, according to which František Maxmilián Kaňka was the most probable designer of this garden. We place the date of its origin in the period after 1717.

The Hartig Garden, with a bower used for music productions originated in the 1720s, as a result of a remodelling of an older, early Baroque garden. In 1965 it was adapted again and connected to the gardens in the southern part of the area below Prague Castle, which were designed by the architect Josef Plečnik. The sculptures on the terrace come from the workshop of Antonín Braun (around 1740), and were brought here from a chateau in Štiřín[74].

The Lesser Quarter of Prague was founded in the valley between the Hradčany, with its architecturally designed terraced gardens, and the northeastern slope of Petřín Hill. Terraced gardens emerged on the Petřín hillside, too, (i.e. the Schönborn and Lobkovic Gardens), but they have not survived in their original Baroque form with architectural elements, though in their time they were among the most famous ones. Only the Vrtba Garden remained in a relatively good condition.

Above left: Malá (Small) Fürstenberg Garden, terraces with stairway, arbours and lookout pavillion
Above centre: Fürstenberg Garden, terraces with stairways and arbours
Above right: Ledebour Garden, terraces with arbour
Page 231: Ledebour Garden, lower stairway

Notes

1. Naňková 1989a, p. 251.

2. Krčálová 1988.

3. Vilímková, M., *Pasport SURPMO* (Documentation), typescript.

4. Chytil, K. Vincenzo Scamozzi v Čechách (Vincenzo Scamozzi in Bohemia). *Ročenka Kruhu*, 1922, 20-60, and 1923, 58.

5. Kašička, F., *Pasport SURPMO* (Documentation), typescript.

6. Preiss 1986, p. 80.

7. Kašička, F., *Pasport SURPMO* (Documentation), typescript.

8. Vlček 1988, p. 494.

9. Vilímková, M., *Pasport SURPMO* (Documentation), typescript.

10. Vlček 1988, p. 494.

11. Preiss 1986, p. 457, note 22.

12. Vlček 1988, figs. 13 ,14, 15, pp. 484, 485, 486.

13. Lancinger, L. and Pavlík, M. 1966. Kostel sv. Maří Magdalény a Francesco Caratti (The Church of St Mary Magdalene and Francesco Caratti. *Umění*, XIV, pp. 109-121, annex.

14. Krčálová 1989, p. 169.

15. Vilímková, M., *Pasport SURPMO* (Documentation), typescript.

16. Lancinger, L. and Pavlík, M. 1966. Kostel sv. Maří Magdalény a Francesco Caratti (The Church of St Mary Magdalene and Francesco Caratti). Umění, XIV, pp. 109-121, annex.

17. Vlček 1984, p. 17, note 4., refs. to 13, 16.

18. Preiss, 1986, p. 173.

19. Pavlík M. and Vilímková, M., *Pasport SURPMO* (Documentation), typescript.

20. Vilímková, M., *Pasport SURPMO* (Documentation), typescript.

21. Vacková, R., Stavba kostela a koleje sv. Ignáce dle plánů(The Construction of the Church and College of St Ignatius according to plans), PA XXXIV, Prague, 1924-5, p. 404 ff.

22. Preiss 1986, p. 361.

23. Archeological excavation was led by Dr Hrdlička of the Archeological Institute of the Czechoslovak Academy of Sciences.

24. Pavlík M. and Lancinger, L., *Pasport SURPMO* (Documentation), typescript.

25. Vlček 1984, p.1.

26. Lancinger, L. and Pavlík, M. 1966. Kostel sv. Maří Magdalény a Francesco Caratti (The Church of St Mary Magdalene and Francesco Caratti). *Umění*, XIV, pp. 109-121, annex.

27. Preiss 1986, p. 230.

28. Lorenc, Tříska, and Uher 1980, p. 77, fig. 50.

29. Sádlo, V. 1935. Kostel sv. Františka u Křižovníků na Starém Městě pražském (The Church of St Francis on the Knights of the Cross Square in the Old Town of Prague). *Ročenka Kruhu* PPDU, p. 42 ff.

30. Preiss 1986, p. 188.

31. Muk, J., *Pasport SURPMO* (Documentation), typescript.

32. Kropáček 1986, pp. 147-150.

33. Vilímková 1986, p. 37, note 45.

34. Pavlík M. and Lancinger, L., *Pasport SURPMO* (Documentation) + appendix, typescript.

35. Lancinger L., Pavlík, M, and Preis P. 1989. *Zámek Trója v Praze* (The Trója Summer Palace in Prague). Prague.

36. Kašička, F. and Vilímková, M., *Pasport SURPMO* (Documentation), typescript.

37. Ibid.

38. Lancinger, L. and Pavlík, M. 1969. Nové prameny k stavebnímu vývoji kostela sv. Josefa pražských karmelitánek a k účasti J.B. Matheye na projektu (New Sources on the Building Development of the Prague Carmelites' Church of St Joseph and the participation of J.B.Mathey in the project). *Umění*, XVII, pp. 357-367.

39. Pavlík, M. and Lancinger, L., *Pasport SURPMO* (Documentation), typescript.

40. Dragoun, Zd. and Sommer, P. 1993. Středověká podoba břevnovského kláštera (The Mediaeval Appearance of the Břevnov Monastery). *Sborník Tisíc let benediktinského kláštera v Břevnově* (Proceedings of the Millenium of the Benedictine Monastery in Břevnov), III, pp. 27, 29. Prague.

41. Blažíček, O.J., Čeřovský, J. and Poche, E. 1944. *Klášter v Břevnově* (The Monastery in Břevnov). Prague.

42. Vilímková and Preiss 1989, pp. 74-86.

43. Ibid.

44. Pavlík, M and Vilímková, M., *Pasport SURPMO* (Documentation), typescript.

45. Vilímková, M. 1969. Ke stavebnímu vývoji komplexu jezuitských budov na Malostranském náměstí (The Building Development of the Jesuit Complex on Lesser Quarter Square). *Umění*, XVII, p. 317 ff.

46. Pavlík, M. and Šíma, J. 1969. Příspěvek k zaklenutí lodi kostela sv. Mikuláše v Praze III (Contributions to the Vaulting of the Nave of the Church of St Nicholas in Prague III), *Umění*, XVII, 1969, p. 76 ff.

47. Pavlík, M. and Vilímková, M., *Pasport SURPMO* (Documentation), typescript.

48. Ibid.

49. Naňková's view is supported by Preiss 1986, p. 302.

50. Preiss 1986, p. 361.

51. Muk, J., *Pasport SURPMO* (Documentation), typescript.

52. Horyna, M., Macek, J., Macek, P. and Preiss, P. 1992. *Oktavián Broggio*. Exhibition catalogue. Litoměřice: Galerie Litoměřic, p. 112 ff.

53. Horyna, M. and Lancinger, L., *Pasport SURPMO* (Documentation), typescript.

54. Horyna, M., Macek, J., Macek, P. and Preiss, P. 1992. *Oktavián Broggio*. Exhibition catalogue. Litoměřice: Galerie Litoměřice, p. 112 ff.

55. Horyna, M. and Lancinger, L., *Pasport SURPMO* (Documentation), typescript.

56. Ibid., axonometry M. Pavlík.

57. Summarized by Preiss 1986, p. 401 and notes 94, 95, 96.

58. Kašička, F. and Vilímková, M., *Pasport SURPMO* (Documentation), typescript.

59. Hyzler, J. and Vilímková, M., *Pasport SURPMO* (Documentation), typescript.

60. Catalogue for the exhibition K.I. Dientzenhofer a umělci jeho okruhu, fig. 62. Prague.

61. Pavlík, M. 1976. Revaloryzacja zespolu pojeznickiego w Pradze. Ochrana zabytków, 3, pp. 165-174.

62. Catalogue for the exhibition K.I. Dientzenhofer a umělci jeho okruhu (K.I. Dientzenhofer and Artists of his Circle), 1989, fig. 165, and the text by Pavel Preiss, p. 178.

63. Hyzler, J. and Vilímková, M., *Pasport SURPMO* (Documentation), typescript.

64. Muk, J., *Pasport SURPMO* (Documentation), typescript.

65. Ibid.

66. Pavlík, M. 1958. Kompozice detailu pražské barokní architektury (Composition of the Detail of Prague Baroque Architecture). *Proceedings of the FAPS conference*. Prague.

67. Pavlík, M. and Lancinger, L., Pasport palácových zahrad pod Hradem (Documentation of the Palace Gardens Below the Castle), SURPMO, typescript.

68. Muk, J. 1990. Poznámky ke stavebnímu vývoji (zahrada Ledeburského paláce) (Notes on the Building Development – Ledebour Garden), SURPMO, typescript for probing the safeguarding project.

69. Pavlík, M. and Lancinger, L., *Pasport SURPMO* (Documentation), typescript.

70. Poche, E. and Preiss, P. 1973. *Pražské paláce* (Prague Palaces). Prague. pp. 67, 68.

71. Macek, P. et alt. 1992, p. 202.

72. Ibid., p. 197.

73. Baseová 1991, p. 214.

74. Ibid., p. 213.

75. Pelzlbauer, V., *Pasport SURPMO* (Documentation), typescript.

76. Macek, P. et alt. 1992, p. 202.

77. Kašička, F., *Pasport SURPMO* (Documentation), typescript.

Bibliography

Bašeová, O. 1991. *Pražské zahrady* (Prague Gardens). Prague: Panorama.

Franz, H. G. 1989. Christoph und Kilian Ignaz Dientzenhofer als Kirchenbaumeister in Prag und Böhmen. *Wiener Jahrbuch für Kunstgeschichte*, XLII, 169-316. Vienna.

Horyna, M., Naňková, V., Pavlík, M. et alt. 1989. *Kilián Ignác Dientzenhofer a umělci jeho okruhu* (Kilián Ignác Dientzenhofer and Artists of His Circle). Prague.

Homolka, J., Hlaváček, I., Horyna, M., Pavlík, M. et alt. 1993. Milénium břevnovského kláštera (The Millennium of the Břevnov Monastery). *Proceedings of the Philosophical Faculty of Charles University*. Prague.

Hubala, E. 1959. Rotunde und Baldachin: Die Raumgliederung der guarinesken Kirchen Böhmens. *Abhandlungen der Braunschweiger wissenschaftlichen Gesellschaft*, XLI.

Kašička, F. 1983. Počátky vyšehradské barokní citadely (The Beginnings of the Vyšehrad Baroque Citadel). *Staletá Praha*, XIII, 191-202.

Krčálová, J. 1988. Giovanni Pieroni – architekt. *Umění*, XXXVI, 511-542.

Krčálová, J. 1989. Renesanční architektura v Čechách a na Moravě (Renaissance Architecture in Bohemia and Moravia). In: *Dějiny českého výtvarného umění* (The History of Czech Visual Arts), II/1, 5-61, 159-181. Prague: Akademia CSAV.

Kropáček, P. 1986. Ke značce architekta J.B. Mathey (The Signature of Architect J.B. Mathey). *Umění*, XXIV, 147-150.

Lorenc, V., Tříska, K., and Uher, V. 1980. *Černínský palác v Praze* (The Černín Palace in Prague). Prague: Panorama.

Macek, P. 1992. *Oktavián Broggio*. Litoměřice: Galerie Litoměřice.

Macek, P., Vlček, P., Zahradník, P., and Kaňka, F.M. 1992. *Umění*, XXXX, 180-227.

Naňková, V. 1986. Review of Heinrich Gerhard Franz, 'Dientzenhofer und "Hausstätter"'. *Umění*, XXXIV, 466-469.

Naňková, V. 1989a. Architektura 17. století v Čechách (17th-century Architecture in Bohemia). In: *Dějiny českého výtvarného umění* (The History of Czech Visual Arts), II/1, 249-278. Prague: Akademia CSAV.

Naňková, V. 1989b. Architektura vrcholného baroka v Praze (High Baroque Architecture in Bohemia). In: *Dějiny českého výtvarného umění* (The History of Czech Visual Arts), II/2, 391-454. Prague: Akademia CSAV.
Norberg-Schulz, C. 1994. *Genius loci*. Prague: Odeon.

Opasek, A.O., Dragoun, Zd., Preiss, P., Pavlík, P. et alt. 1993. *Sborník Tisíc let benediktinského kláštera v Břevnově* (Proceedings of the Millenium of the Benedictine Monastery in Břevnov). Prague.

Poche, E. 1989. Architektura pozdního baroka a rokoka v Čechách (Late-Baroque and Rococo Architecture in Bohemia). In: *Dějiny českého výtvarného umění* (The History of Czech Visual Arts), II/2, 663, 692. Prague: Akademia CSAV.

Preiss, P. 1986. *Italští umělci v Praze* (Italian Artists in Prague). Prague: Panorama.

Sedlák, J. 1987. *Jan Blažej Santini*. Prague: Vyšehrad.

Sperling, I. 1980. Poznámky k restaurátorským pracem ve Valdštejském paláci v Praze (Notes on Restoration Work in the Wallenstein Palace in Prague). *Památky a příroda*, V, 4-13.

Vilímková, M. 1986. *Stavitelé paláců a chrámů* (The Builders of Palaces and Churches). Prague: Vyšehrad.

Vilímková, M., and Preiss, P. 1989. *Ve znamení břevna a růží* (Under the Sign of the Cross-beam and Roses). Prague: Vyšegrad.

Vlček, P. 1984. Francesco Caratti. *Umění*, XXXII, 1-22.

Vlček, P. 1986. Giovanni Domenico Orsi. *Umění*, XXXIV, 416-434.

Vlček, P. 1988. 'Dientzenhoferův skicář' a česká architektura 1640-1670 ('Dientzenhofer's Sketchbook' and Czech Architecture 1640-1670). *Umění*, XXXVII, 473-497.

List of Illustrations

Ornament

The Curve in Plan and Space: Countermovement of Matter

Contrast and Unity

Register

Page 240: The Church of the Holy Trinity, original designs, Ott. Broggio, after 1708